THE COMPLETE BOOK OF FLORENTINE COOKING

Florentine cooking is world famous for its delicious taste and natural ingredients.

Its traditional recipes are tasty, yet of great simplicity.

Certain basic commodities are essential in the preparation of these, such as whole-wheat bread, dried white beans, plum tomatoes, pasta, extra-virgin olive oil, fresh herbs such as rosemary, sage, basil, parsley, wild fennel seeds, chicken livers, and tripe.

Until recently, these staples ingredients have often been hard to find; but now, in most cities around the world, specialized food stores and groceries offer the majority of them, making it possible to reproduce the authentic taste of Florentine cuisine in your home.

This book contains a wide selection of dishes from Florence. All have been **repeatedly tested and adapted to modern kitchen equipment and cooking methods.**

You will also find suggestions, interesting tales, variations and, above all, **the intriguing history of Florence told through its culinary traditions:** from the Etruscans to Catherine de' Medici; from the Grand Dukes of Tuscany to our present day gastronomy.

After decades of success, this best-selling "classic" cookbook has finally been translated into English.
All weights, measurements, instructions and ingredients have been adapted for use in other countries.

Paolo Petroni

The complete book of
FLORENTINE
COOKING

Over 250 traditional recipes
Easy to prepare and delicious to eat

EDIZIONI
IL CENTAURO

Second Edition: October 1997

Printed in Italy
ISBN 88-86540-02-7
Stabilimento Poligrafico Fiorentino
Firenze

Translation and adaptation: Deborah Hodges Maschietto and Paolo Petroni
Text designer: Laura Venturi
Photographs: Roberto Germogli - Firenze

Contents

Introduction

Florentine cooking is tasty and straightforward. It uses simple ingredients, does not require lengthy preparation and is appreciated the world over.

It contains a rich variety of flavours, but the basic ingredients are bread and olive oil. These are used to prepare many varieties of *"crostini"*, *"fettunta"* or *"bruschetta"*, soups such as *"ribollita"*, *"minestra di pane"*, *"zuppa lombarda"* and the delicious *"panzanella"*.

The very same bread and oil are used to make sweet breads such as *"pandiramerino"*, *"schiacciata con l'uva"* and *"schiacciata alla fiorentina"*.

Other typical ingredients are white beans (the exquisite *"fagioli all"uccelletto"*), spinach and Swiss chard used to stuff *"tortellini"*, *"ravioli"*, *"crespelle"* and *"in zimino"*, and cabbage, an essential ingredient for all the vegetable soups.

Tomatoes are almost always included: in the pasta sauces, the stews, the tripe, the *"francesina"*, the *"verdure strascicate"* and the famous *"pappa al pomodoro"*.

Pride of the Florentine cuisine is the renowned, charcoal grilled steak from the local Chianine cattle.

Typical and traditional dishes, ignored by today's cooks, include tongue and hare in sweet-sour sauce. These are distant reminders of the once famed Renaissance cuisine, which was widely influential over the centuries.

In this book, the result of many years research and experimentation, the reader will find a number of recipes used today by families, restaurants and trattorias. Some dishes have been included, which were extremely popular in the past yet are now regrettably forgotten.

These have been chosen on the basis of contemporary taste and slightly adapted in the hope that the reader will be encouraged to try them out.

All the recipes have been tested and their descriptions are simple and clear; allowing an easy and rapid understanding of the ingredients to be used and the procedure to be followed.

Variations, advice, curious facts and historical references are to be found in the notes following most recipes.

Paolo Petroni

Florentine cooking through the centuries

The Etruscan origins

The birth of Florence can be traced back to 59 BC. In that year some of Julius Caesar's veterans founded a colony with the auspicious name of "*Florentia*", that is "flourishing".

These Romans were not, however, the first to covet the green and flowering fields to the right of the Arno, the present day location of the Ponte Vecchio.

Hundreds of years before on the same site, the Etruscans had built a village as an adjunct to the ancient town of Fiesole. This functioned as an outpost for those travelling from North to South; indeed the river was neither wide nor the land marshy at this point.

Name, date and history of that village are today unknown (yet a cemetery dating to about 1000 years before Christ has been found near the church of Orsanmichele); however it is certain that in this Etruscan outpost the long history Florentine cooking first began.

Florence was not yet Florence, but many typical dishes to be found in present day cooking were already carefully and skilfully prepared.

From the frescoes in their tombs, it is clear that the Etruscans used to prepare *pappardelle* (they had the pastry wheel, the colander and the cheese grater), soups, grilled beef steaks and pork chops, barbecued chicken and even *schiacciata* (sweet flat bread) with grapes.

The Etruscans were sophisticated gourmets, they were served by young boys and maidens and they ate whilst reclining and listening to music. They used plates and cups; their food was wholesome and tasty.

After the destruction of this impressive civilisation, one thousand years were to pass before such a gastronomic level was reached once again.

The influence of Rome

By the third century BC, Rome had already conquered a large part of Etruria (Tuscany) and had taken possession of Fiesole and its riverside village.

Thus Florence was first established as a square, walled fortification, not much more than a military camp. However it grew and prospered; during the imperial era (about 22 BC) it constituted the "VII Regio" of Augustus and later in 287 it became the seat of the government of the United Regions of Etruria and Umbria.

Roman Florence with its Forum, Capitol, baths, theatre, amphitheatre and other buildings typical of Roman civilisation, has almost disappeared.

One could say that from the first century BC until the invasion of the barbarians, prior to the fall of the Western Empire (476), Florentine and Roman cooking were much the same thing.

To start with, the alimentation of the Romans was simple and frugal, based essentially upon *"pulmentum"* (barley cooked in broth), *"puls"* (a sort of porridge based on spelt, millet or potato starch), fish, vegetables and cheeses.

With an increase in wealth and dominions, the Romans, like the Etruscans, became excessive in their eating habits, both in quantity and in quality.

Many squandered a fortune in banquets and feasts, prepared with the single aim of amazing guests with courses by the dozen, unusual choreography, ridiculous foods such as peacock brains, flamingo tongue, parrots, dormice, badger, and, an exquisite luxury, the vulva of virgin sow.

Pleasure in good food no longer existed. There remained only its appearance and the ostentation of wealth, the wish to impress one's guests and be the centre of attention.

Naturally, the cooking of the Roman people was not just for special occasions. Evidence of everyday cooking is to be found in *"De re coquinaria"* (About Cooking), a book written by Marco Gavio Apicio, a gastronome living in the time of Tiberius (about 30 AD), wich contained over five hundred recipes.

In this book, he describes many sauces and puddings; he gives advice about improving the taste of food, he cites over sixty spices and flavourings and to each sauce, he adds at least ten.

Today, not one of these recipes has survived. There is perhaps no need for regret considering that almost every dish included *"garum"*, a terribly strong sauce made from a mush of pickled fish entrails.

The feudal period

Whereas excess and indolence characterised Roman life, hordes of famished barbarians pressed in ever closer on the borders of the Empire: it was not long before they spread through Italy.

The Fall of the Roman Empire was followed by a series of invasions: Visigoths, Huns, Vandals, Ostrogoths and Longobards. Florence was heavily attacked by Totila, King of the Ostrogoths (542), but then recovered under Longobard rule and particularly with the wise government of Charlemagne, King of the Franks and founder of the Holy Roman Empire in the year 800.

The continual fear of raids, pestilence, famine and the lack of a central authority resulted in the depopulation of the cities. The people, having fled to the countryside in search of protection from the more powerful lords, favoured feudalism: a primitive form of government characteristic of the Middle Ages.

The feud was like a small state gravitating around the castle: all activities took place within it. Very little money circulated and the taxes were oppressive.

In contrast with the powerful Feudatory, there were hundreds of serfs who lived in the most desperate conditions. Their alimentation included nettle soup, acorns, lizards and mouse pie; documents even deal with episodes of cannibalism.

The situation was quite different within the castle where there was no lack of roast meats, game of every type, fish and vegetables. The meals were, however, monotonous. The food was always the same, full of spices and flavourings and served in no particular order.

The people did not eat, they revelled. There were neither plates not cutlery; a single glass served for all at table. Roasted meats were served on rounds of flat bread, which having exhausted their function as plates, were given to the starving servants. Still soaked in oil and meat juices, they were thrown into a pot together with water, vegetables and flavourings: this was the origin of *crostini* and *ribollita* (bread and vegetable soup).

The division, isolation and lack of communications between these feuds caused the various cooking traditions in Italy to become notably different. The self-sufficient nature of the feudal economy made the use of local resources essential: each region, indeed each area, developed its own specialities, its own typical dishes.

Notwithstanding the passing of almost a thousand years, these peculiarities have remained and still characterise the gastronomic traditions of regions and provinces of Italy today.

The period of the city-states

At the beginning of the 11th century, as though the prophecies concerning the millenium really had come true, life began to improve.

Without fear of barbarian raids, the population, having increased notably in number, began to return to the cities; commercial and industrial activities flourished again (thanks to the Crusades, which had opened the trade routes to the Orient) and the first fairs and markets began to take place.

Florence was the leading Tuscan city, although Lucca in those days was a contender, due to its position as city of transit for those travelling to Rome from the North.

At the end of the 12th century, Florence became an autonomous Free City, at first governed by Counsels and then by the *"Podestà"*. In practice, however, power was in the hands of an oligarchy of powerful and battle-trained families, allies in the famous *"Consorterie delle Torri"* (Consortium of the Towers).

The towers were houses, yet at the same time little fortresses. They were connected by bridges and overhead passages to other house-towers, creating an easily defensible complex. There was no lack of battle: the thirteenth century saw the alternating events of the battle between the Guelphs (followers of the Pope) and the Ghibellines (followers of the Emperor).

In this turbulent period, more importance was given to arms than to food. The kitchens were small and situated at the top of the tower (for fear of fire), the water supplies and the pantry on the ground floor. For the women, it was a continual and exhausting process of going up and downstairs.

Other rooms were also small and if a dinner was organised for many guests, the table was set up in the street, rather like the bars and restaurants of today, which put their tables out on the pavement and in the squares. In this way the neighbours were able to see the abundance and variety of the various courses.

At the beginning of the century, however, the food was still very simple: *fettunta* (toasted bread with garlic and olive oil), *panzanella* (bread and vegetable salad), *ribollita* (vegetable soup), bread soups, *castagnaccio* (chestnut cake) and *pattona* (chestnut porridge).

Bread was cooked in many ways: it even became a pudding. For feasts, in fact, dough was sweetened with honey (sugar was still a rare luxury), grapes, spices and other flavourings, making *panpepato* (bread with pepper), *buccellato* (aniseed cake), *schiacciata* (sweet flat bread) and *pandiramerino* (rosemary buns).

In Dante's time

Notwithstanding the bitter struggles, first between Guelphs and Ghibellines, and later between the Black Guelphs (faithful followers of the Pope) and the White Guelphs (favourable towards the Emperor), it was in the 14th century that the great Florentine civilisation fully matured.

Florence became a true state, able to deal on an equal basis with kings and popes; it was the centre of international culture, leader in the arts, literature, language and customs.

Eating and cooking habits also reflected this period of ferment and renovation: kitchens became more spacious and those who could, built a large fireplace. The preparation of food became more refined. In the first half of the 14th century, a new instrument began to be used for eating: the fork. This piece of tableware was to remain unknown in the rest of Italy for many years to come and for even longer in France, where it only began to be used in the 16th century.

It is comprehensible, therefore, that the great poet Dante Alighieri, as a White Guelph, suffered so much when forced to leave his beloved Florence in 1302.

The shops sold everything: Florentine olive oil, beef from the Val di Chiana, chickens, lamb and vegetables of every type, even ready-boiled greens and spinach, just like today.

There were fish of every type, not just from the river Arno, which were delicious and abundant (the little fried fish from the Arno were, up until the last century, the boast of numerous Florentine restaurants), but also sea fish, like red mullet, grey mullet, gilt-head bream, cuttlefish, prawns and shrimps. More fish was eaten then than now; perhaps because both Fridays and Saturdays were considered meatless (abstinence) days at that time.

The fish market was near Ponte Vecchio, in the present day piazza del Pesce (Fish Square). In this little square there was an open gallery called "Loggia dei pesciaiuoli" (Fishmongers' loggia) later demolished by Cosimo I de' Medici to make room for the construction of the Vasari corridor (a passage joining Palazzo Vecchio to the Pitti palace, built over the Ponte Vecchio).

The fish sellers were transferred to the Mercato Vecchio (Old Market), now piazza della Repubblica, where Vasari built the famous "Loggia del Pesce": this in turn was destroyed during the rebuilding of the city centre (1885), and was recently moved to via Pietrapiana.

Notwithstanding the lack of refrigeration, the fish was always fresh because covered with ice from the underground ice-houses.

In these useful cellars, ice was kept from the winter, and used to cool drinks: indeed ice cold drinks have always been a great passion of the Florentines.

14th century cooking habits

A cookery book, written at the beginning of the 14th century by a Tuscan, perhaps Florentine, cook, includes 57 recipes, many of which are still used today.

Here we find: *ravioli, tortelli, maccheroni* (these were perhaps our present day *gnocchi* (dumplings) made with wheat flour), *pasticci* or *timballi* (meat pies); duck, capons and crane; stewed shoulder of mutton and marinated ox head.

We find fish from the Arno including lamprey, eel, crayfish and tench; leek pies, spinach and Swiss chard pies and "white food": various preparations, both sweet and savoury, based on cream, rice, chopped boiled chicken breast, sugar, rose and orange water.

Finally dessert: *pinocchiati* (pine nut cookies), *confetti* (sugared almonds), marzipan, *treggea* (small coloured sugared almonds), quince, apple and pumpkin preserves.

Apart from these delicious and tasty foods, there were others which today's palate has a little difficulty in appreciating. In particular, there was the common use of the *"dolceforte"* (sweet-sour), in other words, the combination of fruit, such as grapes, plums, apples and chestnuts with meat and fish.

In all these dishes, there were spices in large quantities to mask the rather strong taste of the meat, which began to go off quite quickly.

This is the main reason for the exaggerated use of spices and flavourings in past cooking techniques. Today, these are used far less and when they are, it is to give a particular flavour to a dish, not to cover the odour of incipient putrefaction.

The Council of Florence

The continuing battles between rival families and contrasts between the bourgeoisie and proletariat soon caused the Free City to fall in favour of an authoritarian government which guaranteed stability.

After the unfortunate experience of the Signoria of the Duke of Athens (a French adventurer kicked out of Florence in 1343) and the ephemeral people's government, which rose out of the "Rebellion of the Ciompi" (workers and wool carders) in 1378, an oligarchic government was formed of members of the powerful families of bankers and merchants (Strozzi, Pitti, Pazzi, Albizi, Antinori, Medici, Tornabuoni, etc.).

Of the two most prominent families, the Medici prevailed over the Albizi due to the wisdom and ability of Cosimo de' Medici, called "The Elder", who became Signore of the city (1434).

Brilliant, shrewd and in love with his city, Cosimo did much for Florence and certainly deserved the title of *"Padre della Patria"* (Father of his Country) which he was given after his death.

To give further importance to his city, Cosimo convinced the Pope to move the Ecumenical Council of the Greek and Roman Churches to Florence. This had been inaugurated in Ferrara in 1438 and on 27th January 1439, the Pope (Eugene IV) and his court entered Florence. Everything was funded by the Banca de' Medici.

There were great banquets and feasts; the splendour, the fun-loving and sophisticated lifestyle in Florence was discussed throughout the known world.

Legend has it that during the course of the Council two words were used for the first time which were destined to remain an essential part of Florentine cuisine: *"Arista"* and *"Vin Santo"*.

Arista will be discussed in the meat chapter, whereas here below is an anecdote concerning the origins of the word Vin Santo (Holy wine).

One day the Greek cardinal Bessarione was given to taste sweet wine or *"vin pretto"*, as it was then called. As soon as he tasted this, he is said to have exclaimed: "But this is Xantos!", alluding to a similar wine produced on the Greek island of the same name.

Those who heard him (the word Xantos sounds like the Italian term "santo", which means "holy") thought that he referred to the sacred quality of the wine and so, from that day on, the name has stuck.

According to another, less amusing yet probably truer, version, it seems that this wine had been called "santo" from time immemorial, priests having always preferred this sweet wine for celebrating Mass.

However, even if the Council invented no new names, it brought fame and resonance to Florence. Cosimo, as befitted his role as Signore of the city, had a new and splendid palace built in via Larga (now Cavour St.).

Here he hosted many feasts which, although not over extravagant, always included abundant choice of dishes, served and cooked to perfection. The settings were carefully prepared and the courses followed a precise order, very similar to that of today, except for some sweets, such as the *pinocchiati*, which were sometimes served as hors d'oeuvres.

Lorenzo the Magnificent

Cosimo the Elder died in 1464 and was succeeded for a brief period by his mediocre son, Piero, called "il gottoso" (the Gouty), a disease wich had afflicted a great many of the Medici family. In 1469, the son of Piero, Lorenzo, became Signore of the City.

Only twenty years old, he knew how to govern Florence with a strict yet reasonable rule. He surrounded himself with literary figures, making Florence the lively centre of humanist thought.

Lorenzo encouraged man to centre his attention not only on God, as mediaeval culture commanded, but also on the concrete problems of earthly existence. Inviting neither an exasperated individualism nor a pagan indifference to the supreme values of life, Lorenzo "winked" and gave his advise: "Be merry today, for tomorrow's fate is uncertain ...".

As a natural accompaniment to this philosophy, Lorenzo appreciated good food and to judge from the amorous-gastronomic rhymes he wrote in his poem the "Nencia da Barberino", held it in high regard notwithstanding his skinny and minute frame.

Nencia (perhaps his girlfriend) was whiter than *"fior di farina"* (flour), *"saporita che non il cacio"* (tastier than cheese) and *"morbida che par un migliaccio"* (as soft as a chestnut cake).

In his "Canto de' Cialdonai" (Canto of the Cornet Makers), Lorenzo also proved to be a good cook.

Lorenzo died at only 44 years old (1492), prematurely aged and saddened by the continual threats and pressing appeals for austerity, which the Black Friar Girolamo Savonarola did not tire of preaching to the Florentines from the pulpit of the San Marco church.

The son of Lorenzo, Piero, (known as "the fatuous" or "the unfortunate") was soon defeated by the sermons of the Dominican monk from Ferrara, who wished for a republican government of theocratic inspiration.

But the success of Savonarola was to be short lived; his ascetic ideals belonged to Mediaeval culture and soon began to tire the Florentines. They changed sides and the Pope Alexander VI seized the opportunity to excommunicate the monk, who had become a real nuisance with his obsessive invectives.

On 23rd May 1498, after an unjust trial held only for appearances, Girolamo Savonarola was hanged and burnt as a heretic in piazza della Signoria. The Florentines, oppressed by the weight of his austerity, did not weep his death; indeed many inns and butchers opened their doors to the public as life began to seep back into the city.

The Discovery of America

The discovery of the American continent (1492) was fundamental for the Florentine cuisine: many different products reached Italy from that far away land, which were profoundly to change the face of Italian gastronomy.

Florence, for some time an artistic and commercial centre, was to be amongst the first European cities to taste beans, potatoes, tomatoes, corn (maize), chocolate and turkey from across the Atlantic.

The bean received such a welcome, it seemed that this city had always been aware of its existence and expecting its arrival; as though until then they had accepted a substitute, whilst awaiting the real king of the table.

A particular type of bean had in fact existed in Florence before the discovery of America; Lorenzo the Magnificent reminds his reader that after a plate of beans "sgonfiar bisogna" (one must break wind). These were neither white (haricot) beans (Phaseolus vulgaris) nor red (kidney) ones, but those known as "black-eyed beans" which, notwithstanding their appearance, are not beans at all.

Real beans reached the Florentine table at the beginning of the 16th century, perhaps in the form of a gift to the Florentines from Pope Clement VII (Giulio de' Medici), who in turn had received them as a present from the Emperor of Spain, Charles V.

Renaissance Feasts

From a political point of view, the beginning of the 16th century was not so fortunate for Florence. In 1529, as an ally of the King of France, Frances I, it experienced the only real siege in its history by the Emperor of Spain Charles V.

With its capitulation, notwithstanding numerous heroic acts (including the sacrifice of Francesco Ferrucci), Florence lost its old freedom and became a state governed by a hereditary and absolute government.

Pope Clement VII (Medici) crowned the Emperor Charles V and in exchange requested that the Medici become Signori of Florence.

He obtained much more: in 1531 his illegitimate son, Alexander, entered the city with the official title of first Duke of Florence. He could not have asked for more.

Alexander de' Medici, violent and dissolute, introduced an affected and refined cuisine to the palace on via Larga (today Cavour St.). His Renaissance style feasts are still famous today for their excess, exaggeration, waste and vulgar and disturbing choreography.

The many courses included certain hors d'oeuvres which, had they not been followed by an extraordinary number of other courses and accompanied by various scenes in bad taste, resembled almost identically certain present day dishes.

The cold courses included: carrots, chicory, capers, endive, green and mixed salads, and then sausages, brains, sweetbreads, fried meatballs or meatballs in sauce, ham and salami.

There were a large variety of sauces: green sauce, bitter-sweet, peppery, sour grape, pine nut, etc.

There was naturally no lack of wild boar, pheasant and peacock dressed in their own skin or feathers. Many paintings and movies have presented these as symbols of those exaggerated 16th century feasts. However, they were no novelty: the Romans had also prepared such feasts but neither they, nor the Renaissance guests, ever ate them; in fact the cooks needed so long to decorate them that in the meantime they has usually decomposed and had often to be sprinkled with sweet smelling essences and spices to mask their stink.

Contemporary writers and poets were not immune to this passion for gastronomic choreography. Amongst those to write in favour, the most important was the "non-Florentine" Pietro Aretino (from Arezzo). In just a few lines, he synthesised the importance and greatness of the Florentine cuisine:

"... setting the table, decorating this with roses, washing the glasses, adding the plums to the stew (sweet-sour sauces), wrapping the pig's liver with caul, making the chestnut cakes and serving fruit at the end of the meal; these all came from Florence. The Florentines have intelligently understood how to entice those with poor appetite."

Catherine de' Medici

Another important recognition of Florentine cuisine came from the French.

Their gastronomic tradition is based largely on the teaching of the Florentine cooks in the court of Catherine de' Medici (daughter of Lorenzo II, Duke of Urbino and granddaughter of Lorenzo the Magnificent).

These cooks accompanied her to Paris, where she was sent, at only fourteen years old, as intended wife of Henry of Orleans, the future Henry II (1533).

On the influence of Florentine culture imposed by Catherine and her cooks and bakers on the French court, Flammarion wrote:

"We must recognise that the Italian cooks who came to France with Catherine de' Medici, at the time of her marriage to Henry II, were at the origins of the French cuisine. For its elements and condiments were for the French a novelty. Our cooks (La Varenne, De Masseliet, Valet, De La Chapelle, Careme and Escoffier) were greatly inspired by these and it did not take them long to surpass their initiators".

Catherine, an enthusiastic eater and heavy drinker, brought to France sauces (including the "glue" ,which became béchamel sauce), giblets, roast birds in orange sauce, crepes, olive oil, the art of frying and the newly introduced white beans. She introduced the use of spinach (recipes called "Florentine style" are prepared with spinach and béchamel), peas and artichokes.

With reference to artichokes and giblets, the chronicles tell that in 1576, during a wedding banquet, she ate so much *"cibreo"* (see the recipe) with artichokes that "one thought she would collapse".

Antonin Careme himself, the famous cook and father of the great French cuisine, admitted in 1822:

"The cooks of the second half of the 17th century knew the taste of the Italian cuisine which Catherine de' Medici had introduced to the French court."

Jean Orieux, in his volume dedicated to Catherine, wrote about the "revolution" of 1533 and stated that:

"The Florentines had reformed the ancient French cuisine of mediaeval tradition; it is from their experience that modern French cuisine originates."

The Grand Dukes of Tuscany

With the slaying of the tyrannical Duke Alexander, killed by his cousin Lorenzino de' Medici (1537), the long reign of the descendents of Cosimo, "Father of his Country", came to an end.

Due to the lack of direct heirs, Cosimo I, son of Giovanni delle Bande Nere, (a famous soldier of the Medici family but descendent of Lorenzo, the brother of Cosimo the Elder), was nominated the Duke of Florence.

Cosimo I took power in a very difficult moment for the Florentine and Tuscan economies but he knew how to rule with severity and firm authority and managed to turn the fortunes of Florence.

The new Duke encouraged agriculture, reclaimed marshy lands and planted olive groves and vineyards, preparing the characteristics of the present day Chianti area.

Interested in botany, Cosimo cultivated rare plants in his Boboli Gardens in Pitti Palace (this palace was bought by his wife, Eleanor of Toledo, in 1549).

These included the mulberry tree, miniature pears and other exotic varieties of fruit trees. The other newly introduced plants, potatoes and tomatoes (originally from Peru), were already well diffused (especially fried) in Florence, whereas in other parts of North Italy, they were still considered purely ornamental.

The luxurions and extravagant feasts of Alexander seemed only a vague memory, yet one could eat well in Florence. Reading Jacopo Carrucci, a famous painter called il "Pontormo", in his diaries written between 1554 and 1555, one finds the typical menu of a present day Florentine trattoria.

Amongst the foods eaten by the artist, were pea soup, mutton soup, kid's head, caviar, rosemary buns, boiled meat served with butter, asparagus with eggs, "pecorino" cheese with fresh broad (fava) beans, eggs and artichokes, roast meats, fried eggs, boiled pigeons, boiled lamb's kidney, boiled beef, boiled, marrow and then plums, walnuts, raisins and figs

Notwithstanding his undeniable merits, Cosimo was not loved by the Florentines during the 37 years of his government. The climate of terror, the draining taxes and the high prices of basic goods suffocated the positive aspects of his administration, which undoubtedly brought a new splendour to Florence.

After a lengthy and wise diplomatic process, Cosimo I managed to have himself crowned the Grand Duke of Tuscany (1569) by the Pope Pio V, thus becoming the most powerful sovereign in Italy.

Marie de' Medici

At his death, the title of Grand Duke passed to his two sons, first to Francis I (1574) and then, at his demise (which took place in his mansion house of Poggio a Caiano in mysterious circumstances) to Ferdinand I (1587).

With these two Grand Dukes, the luxury and sophistication of the beginning of the century returned. There were many banquets and feasts but of all these, the most famous remained that given by Ferdinand I on occasion of the wedding of his niece, Marie de' Medici (daughter of Francis I and of Joanna of Austria), to the King of France, Henry IV (who, in order to marry Marie, divorced the famous Margot, daughter of Catherine). It is said to have been the richest in the history of Florence.

The wedding took place by Proxy and the nuptial banquet took place on 5th October 1600 in the Salone dei Cinquecento (Hall of the Five Hundred) in Palazzo Vecchio, organised by Bernard Buontalenti for three hundred guests.

The list of the courses began with 24 cold dishes, amongst these: mixed salads, veal and wild boar pies, ox tongue, pigeon, chicken, lamprey and so on.

There then followed 18 hot courses (quail, chicken, pheasant, capon) and yet another 10 hot courses (thrush, lark, pork, partridge, etc.), then pudding, ice-cream, cheese, vegetables and peaches in wine.

At the beginning of the 17th century, life was peaceful and there were no more cruel fights for power. In the streets of the city, people could stop and chat in peace and in the bars, they could sip the new drink, the "*cioccolatte*" (chocolate with milk), which the Florentine merchant, Francesco Carletti, had brought back from one of his long journeys to South America.

In the same period, the architect Buontalenti dug some ice-rooms under the gardens of Florence, and particularly in the via delle Ghiacciaie (Icehouse St.).

In this street, as Ugo Pesci recounts in his book "Florence Capital": "There were vast rectangles under the street level, called "ice-houses", into which, in winter, water was allowed to enter up to a certain level; in this way ice was made and even skated on."

Thanks to this ice and to the snow from the surrounding hills which was kept, well pressed down, in the cellars, everybody was able to enjoy the first sorbets in history (made with iced milk and honey).

Marie de' Medici and her alchemist Ruggieri then took these to France, where they were given the name "*cherbert*", or sorbet.

But the second Medici queen not only taught the French cooks how to make ice-cream: she also revealed the secret of making shortcrust pastry, custard, and the fritter batter.

From a gastronomic point of view, the French really owe a great deal to the Florentine queens.

The end of the Medici

Ferdinand I died in 1609 and was succeeded by his son, Cosimo II. The latter, ill with an ulcer, tuberculosis and gout, closed down the famous Bank of the Medici (he did not feel it dignified for a sovereign to be dealing in money) and dispersed a great deal of his inheritance in charity.

The situation was not improved when, after his premature death (1621), his son Ferdinand II became Grand Duke at the age of 10, given that the government remained in the hands of his grandmother, the authoritarian and bigoted Mary Christine of Lorraine.

Life at court was melancholy, but the city did not feel the same way and even the brother of the Grand Duke, the Cardinal Gian Carlo, a great gourmet, continued to entertain.

During those years French names were given to Florentine recipes (tuna fish sauce was called "au thon") and to employ a French cook was a sign of distinction.

With the death of his father (1670), Cosimo III became Grand Duke.

He was also ill, obsessively religious, blatantly betrayed by his wife, of unpleasant appearance and homosexual. He held Florencein a state of mysticism, took the prostitutes off the streets but in compensation, beggars, and thieves invaded Florence.

When Cosimo died (1723), the third son, Gian Gastone, came to the throne with the certainty of being the last Grand Duke of Tuscany.

Victim of an unhappy marriage and homosexual, he had no children. The dynasty of the Medici, which had decided the fate of Florence for over three hundred years, came to an undignified end.

The Dukes of Lorraine

On the death of Gian Gastone, the Grand Duchy of Tuscany was assigned by the European powers participating at the Peace of Vienna (1738), to Francis III of Lorraine (Francis II as Grand Duke of Tuscany). He did not particularly appreciate his new title since, having married Marie Theresa of Austria, daughter of the Emperor Charles VI, he knew that sooner or later he would become Emperor himself.

The new Duke came to Florence unwillingly. A triumphal Arch was erected in his honour in piazza San Gallo (today Libertà Sq.) and he was welcomed with merry celebrations. Nevertheless he remained only a short time (from January to April 1739): with the death of his father-in-law, he returned to

Vienna, leaving Florence in the hands of an unsatisfactory regency.

On his death (in the meantime he had become Emperor of Austria as Francis I) he was succeeded by his second son, Peter Leopold (1765), who was a strict but good ruler. In 1790 he left Florence to become Emperor.

His son, Ferdinand III, remained but he was forced to leave Florence in 1799, driven out by Napoleon and the French army.

For a brief period, Tuscany was part of the French Empire (the sister of Napoleon, Elise Baciocchi, appointed herself Grand Duchess of Tuscany) but then, after the fall of Napoleon, the Grand Duke was able to return to the city.

At his death in 1824, he was succeeded by his son, Leopold II , affectionately named "Canapone" (Big Hemp) for his big white moustache.

Loved and admired by all, Tuscany underwent a new period of prosperity after the unfortunate government by the French, which had sucked the finances of the state quite dry.

They had, in exchange, left behind their refined language, their sophisticated manners and culinary expressions, many of which are still used in our gastronomic vocabulary today. The trattoria became *"restaurant"*, the list of dishes, *"menu"*, the sideboard *"buffet"*, the broth, *"consommé"*, the sweet, *"dessert"*, an evening reception, *"soirée"*. All the recipes were "à la Florentine" and the aperitif was taken at the *"café"*.

The menu of the official dinners at Palazzo Vecchio were almost entirely written in French, the wines and liqueurs were only French and no traditional Florentine recipe was served to foreign guests.

Florence, the Capital of the Italian Kingdom

Times changed quickly: the wars of independence pushed Canapone out and Florence became part of the Kingdom of Italy (1860). In 1865 Florence became the provisory capital of the Kingdom, but the advantages proved to be far less than the disadvantages.

The expenses of adapting the city were enormous and the debts amounted by the Commune of Florence have still not been completely paid. The city also suffered artistically: the walls were pulled down (and substituted with the boulevards), beautiful convents and palaces were destroyed.

The old centre of the city was completely gutted in 1885 and the Old Market, with its sellers of lamb's heads, salt cod fish, herrings, its typical restaurants and trattorias selling frogs, tripe and sweetbreads, was to completely disappear together with the beautiful buildings and mediaeval churches.

There was no doubt that a central city clean-up was necessary; the filthy conditions in which people were forced to live were not compatible with a city such as Florence. Yet as so often happened in these circumstances, the operation was exaggerated and all these problems were resolved by destroying the old city centre.

A fervid supporter of this operation (he also wrote a famous article called *"Firenze sotterranea"* (Underground Florence)) was the journalist, Giulio Piccini, known with the pen-name of Jarro.

He was an enthusiastic eater, a gastronome and refined cook, he published many recipes, often of his own invention, in the *"Almanacchi gastronomici"* (Gastronomic almanacs), published every Christmas.

His recipes which were very elaborate, difficult to realise and far from the simple tastes of normal families, did not meet with great success.

Pellegrino Artusi

A contemporary of Jarro, Pellegrino Artusi, who originated from Romagna, born on 4th August 1820 in Forlimpopoli, but lived nearly all his life in Florence, in piazza d'Azeglio, wrote a book in 1891, which was to become a milestone in the history of cooking books: *"La scienza in cucina e l'arte di mangiare bene"* (Science in the kitchen and the art of eating well).

This is still, after all these years, one of the most essential and popular cooking books (to think that Artusi could find no-one to print it). Finally, he paid for it himself; it was published in Florence by Salvadore Landi, Director of the Arte della Stampa, and the book could only be bought from the author himself by mail.

Artusi wrote this book as an antithesis to the invading French cuisine particularly encouraged by King Vittorio Emanuele II, who greatly appreciated French cooking, in which butter dominated over exquisite Florentine olive oil.

The book was a clamorous success, if not immediately, and thousands of copies (and then millions) were sold. Artusi became a rich man and died satisfied at 91 years old in 1911.

The influence of this book was enormous; for the first time a single, complete, well researched and well written text dealt with Italian cooking.

Women, even those in more financially comfortable positions, began to cook themselves and receive an enthusiastic response from their children and husbands.

Florence today

Since then, two world wars have taken place and much has changed: the intense pace of today's life leaves little time for lengthy and complicated recipes.

Concerns about weight and diet cause people to view some of the traditional recipes with suspicion, considering them to be heavy and indigestible.

By constantly reducing the ingredients and searching for something simple and easy, the number of traditional Florentine dishes have notably decreased in recent years.

The menus of many Florentine restaurants include only a few dishes: *crostini, ribollita, penne strascicate,* Florentine steaks, roast pork, *tripe,* beans, *torta della nonna, tiramisù* and *Prato bisquit.*

The typical sweet-sour sauces, the eel, the timbale and the pheasant with truffles have completely disappeared.

The many soups and *minestroni,* the stews, the *francesina,* the *inzimino* of cuttlefish, the tripe, the salt cod with leeks and many other dishes are hard to find.

Even if certain complicated recipes are no longer possible (whole wheat country bread is now rare), even if the fish from the Arno exist no more, the real Florentine cuisine is as inviting and tasty as ever.

Many of its components have improved over the years. Above all: Tuscan wines have made incredible progress and, both red and white, are excellent and now amongst the best in Italy.

The extra virgin olive oil has reached notable levels of quality and delicacy, even though prices have unfortunately risen..

Finally, after the decline in the "minimal" and pretentious dishes of the *"nouvelle cuisine",* we have returned to typical and traditional recipes. These have often been re-interpreted with creativity in presentation, up-to-date cooking suggestions and a few variations in keeping with modern taste and diet.

Antipasti
Starters,
Hors d'oeuvre

Agli sott'aceto
Pickled garlic

Ingredients

- Large, fresh garlic
- White wine vinegar
- Sage
- Peppercorns
- Salt

- Choose the largest and plumpest cloves of fresh Elephant garlic (not more than one month old). These will have a less pungent taste.
- Peel and place in an earthenware jar (light will cause the garlic to darken). Lightly salt and cover with high quality white wine vinegar.
- Add some leaves of fresh sage (or basil) and peppercorns.
- Leave to infuse. They will be ready after four weeks.
- These garlic cloves are delicious as starters or with boiled meat.

With this preparation, the garlic mellows and loses all its mordant flavour, and will therefore have no unpleasant effect on digestion or breath.

If you do not have an earthenware jar, use a glass jam jar and wrap it with aluminium foil to protect the garlic from the light.

Cipolle sott'aceto
Pickled onions

Ingredients

- Red onions
- Red wine vinegar
- Red wine
- Bay leaves
- Black peppercorns

- 2 cloves
- A sprig of thyme
- A piece of cinnamon
- Salt

- Peel off the outer skin of the onions and then place in a glass jar.
- Boil the vinegar for a few minutes with two cups of red wine, a little salt and all the herbs and spices, then pour over the onions until completely covered.
- Leave to cool, then seal the jar and infuse for at least a month before eating.

The perfect onion for this recipe is oval in shape, but you can also use shallots or normal round onions, as long as they are small and red (boiling onions).

The vinegar should be made the traditional way with good red wine.

These onions are an ideal starter as they stimulate the secretion of gastric juices.

In Florence, there was a popular saying: "This is the month of onions!", in other words, a period without work. In fact the onions sprout in the months of July and August, coinciding with the period in which many craftsmen had less work.

Coccoli
Bread dough fritters

Ingredients for 6 persons

- Plain flour:
  450 g/ 1 lb/ 4 cups
- Cake yeast:
  15 g/ ½ oz/ 1 cake
- A little broth or milk

- Lard or butter:
  30g/ 1 oz/ 2 tablespoons
- Salt
- Oil for frying

- Sift the flour, shape it into a mound and make a well in the centre.
- Dissolve the yeast in a cup of lukewarm broth or milk, add some salt and pour into the well.
- Add the softened lard or butter and knead together to form a smooth and elastic dough.
- Shape into a ball and leave to rise for a couple of hours.
- Take little pieces of the dough (flour your hands) and make small balls about 2 cm/ ¾ inch in diameter, then deep fry in plenty of hot oil.
- When the "coccoli" are puffed up and golden, drain on some paper towels and serve hot, sprinkled with salt. They are delicious!

To speed up the preparation, some baking powder (without vanilla or sugar) can be used in place of the yeast but in this case, there is no need to leave the dough to stand.
The term "coccoli" comes from the "coccola", the round berry of the cypress.

Popular fried bread dough

Fried dough has always been very popular in Florence and in Tuscany in general.

By spreading out the dough with a rolling pin to about ½ cm/ ¼ inch thick and cutting it into "diamonds", you can make the famous "crescentine".

"Panzanelle", "Panzerotti" and "Ficattole" are all bread dough fritters with different shapes from different parts of Tuscany.

Collo ripieno
Stuffed chicken neck

Ingredients for 6 persons

- 2 chicken necks
- Ground (minced) beef:
  200 g/ 7 oz
- Ground (minced) pork:
  100 g/ 3 oz
- Grated Parmesan cheese:
  30 g/ 1 oz/ 4 tablespoons
- Butter: 50 g/ 2 oz/ ¼ cup
- 3 eggs
- Breadcrumbs
- Nutmeg
- Thyme
- Salt and pepper
- Broth

- Pluck the chicken necks thoroughly, and eliminate the neck bone (your butcher can do this, on request).
- Place the ground beef and pork in a sauté pan and cook in the butter flavoured with thyme. Leave to cool, then pass through a food mill or put in a food processor fitted with steel blades, to obtain a smooth mixture.
- Add the eggs, cheese, 4 tablespoons of breadcrumbs, a little nutmeg, salt and pepper. Mix well.
- Stuff the chicken necks, but not too full, tie up with string at both ends and boil in hot broth.
- Simmer over a very low heat for about half an hour, the water should never actually boil, otherwise the necks might break. Turn the heat off and leave the necks to cool down in the broth.
- Cut the necks into thick round slices and serve with pickles.

Do not use the chicken livers in the stuffing as these will give an unpleasant taste. However, chopped parsley, a little garlic and a small quantity of grated lemon peel can be added.

Coccoli

Ribollita

Crostini di fegatini
Chicken livers on toast

Ingredients for 6 people

- Chicken livers:
  300 g/ 11 oz
- ½ onion
- 2 salted anchovy fillets
- 1 tablespoon capers
- A little white wine
- A little broth
- Butter
- Olive oil
- Salt and pepper
- Whole-wheat bread

- Chop the onion finely and sauté in 4 tablespoons of oil until transparent, add the perfectly cleaned chicken livers.
- Stir frequently while slowly adding a little wine.
- After about a quarter of an hour, remove from heat and chop finely on a chopping board (or in a food processor with steel blades).
- Transfer to the pan, add 2 tablespoons of butter, the finely chopped capers and the well cleaned anchovy fillets, season with salt and pepper and cook for a quarter of an hour, adding a little broth at a time.
- Cut slices of bread about 6 mm/ ¼ inch thick, toast them and lightly dip one side only into the broth, spread the still warm mixture onto the dry side of the toasted bread

---

The many ways of preparing "crostini"

Crostini is a typical Florentine antipasto, it is served in all restaurants and trattorias. I have never tasted the same crostini in any two restaurants: they all differ, sometimes in only a subtle way. Not always, however, are they prepared as they should be.

Quite apart from the proportions of the ingredients, the most usual variations consist in the addition of celery, carrot, parsley and a little tomato sauce.

There are also various types of bread used. Some use whole-wheat Tuscan bread (the most typical) and some white baguette-like bread; there are those who fry it in oil or butter, and others who serve it in its natural state.

Follow your individual taste, but for me, the classic solution is the best: take whole-wheat bread, a couple of days old, cut into slices about 6 mm/ ¼ inch high, slightly toast and dip quickly into broth.

Crostini di fegatini e milza
Chicken livers and veal spleen on toast

Ingredients for 6 people

- Chicken livers: 150 g/ 5 oz
- Veal spleen: 200 g/ 7 oz
- Butter: 50 g/ 1¾ oz/ ¼ cup
- ½ onion
- White wine
- 1 tablespoon capers

- 4 salted anchovy fillets
- Broth
- Olive oil
- Salt and pepper
- Bread

- Finely chop the onion and sauté in a little oil until slightly golden, then add the clean and roughly chopped chicken livers.
- Sauté for a little, then baste with half a cup of white wine and allow this to evaporate completely
- Add the paste of the spleen (having removed the skin with the blunt edge of a knife), the chopped capers and the cleaned anchovy fillets.
- Lightly salt and pepper, and cook for about 40 minutes, occasionally adding a little hot broth.
- Take half of the mixture and chop quite finely on a chopping board with a knife. Pass the rest through a food mill or puree in a food processor with steel blades.
- Put this altogether into a saucepan and add the butter. Bring to the boil and the mixture is ready.
- Meanwhile, prepare the bread as follows: cut slices about 6 mm/ ¼ inch thick and toast slightly.
- Taking the slices, dip one side only into the hot broth and spread the mixture on the dry side.

Crostini di milza
Veal spleen on toast

Ingredients for 6 people

- Veal spleen: 350 g/2 oz
- ½ onion
- 4 salted anchovy fillets
- 1 tablespoon capers
- 1 cup red wine

- A little broth
- Butter
- Olive oil
- Salt and pepper
- Bread

- Sauté the finely chopped onion in 2 tablespoons of butter and 2 of olive oil until it begins to turn golden, then add the spleen, having removed its skin with the blunt edge of a knife.
- Cook for a little and then add the red wine, which will help loosen the spleen from the bottom of the pan.
- Reduce, then add the cleaned anchovy fillets and the chopped capers. Salt and pepper slightly and continue to cook over a low heat for a few minutes, basting with some broth, if necessary.
- This should result in a creamy mixture, which is spread on the bread, previously toasted and dipped on one side only into the broth (the mixture should be spread on the dry side).

Fagioli e caviale
Caviar and beans

Ingredients

- White (haricot) beans
- Caviar
- Lemon
- Extra virgin olive oil
- Salt
- Pepper in a grinder

- Cook the beans as usual, and leave to cool in their water.
- Place in a dish (four spoonfuls per person), then add the caviar (1 teaspoon per person), very good olive oil, a few drops of lemon juice, a little salt and plenty of freshly ground pepper.

This recipe was invented by the founders of the Paoli restaurant in via Tavolini in Florence (established in 1824 by Pietro Paoli and his son, Cesare). The aim was to make the beans, normally served with tuna fish, herrings or anchovies, a more dignified dish.

Fettunta or Bruschetta
Garlic toast

Ingredients

- Whole-wheat bread
- Garlic
- Extra virgin olive oil
- Salt
- Pepper in a grinder

- Cut the bread (with its crust) into slices about a finger thick and toast over hot charcoals (preferably made of olive wood). The bread should be crunchy and well-grilled on both sides but soft in the middle.
- While still hot, rub one side with a clove of garlic; salt lightly, sprinkle with

freshly ground pepper and plenty of olive oil. This must be Italian (Tuscan) extra virgin olive oil and, if possible, newly pressed.

- Eat immediately while hot and crunchy.

The origins of this *"pan unto"* (oiled bread), also known as *"bruschetta"* , are obvious: it has been served to hungry families who, either due to famine or poverty, had nothing else to eat.

Today it is a fashionable snack or starter, popular for its traditional origins and its genuine ingredients and taste.

Another way to enjoy *"fettunta"* is to cover it with boiled white beans.

Insalata di Caterina
Catherine's salad

Ingredients

- Mixed green salad (lettuce, chicory, corn salad, etc.)
- Tuscan soft "pecorino" (sheep's milk cheese)
- Eggs (½ per person)
- Anchovy fillets in oil
- Capers
- Vinegar
- Olive oil
- Salt and pepper

- Wash the different varieties of salad (at least three), dry well and place in a large salad bowl (a wooden bowl is ideal and typical for this dish).
- Add the "pecorino" cut into small cubes, little pieces of anchovy fillet and a few capers.
- Salt, pepper lightly and dress with oil and vinegar, toss well and serve immediately, decorated with wedges of hard boiled eggs.

*This delicious salad takes its name from Catherine of the Medici (it was one of her favourite dishes) and is also known as **"Misticanza del pastore"** (shepherd's mixture) or **"Insalata rinascimentale"**(Renaissance salad).*

Insalata di trippa
Tripe salad

Ingredients for 6 people

- Boiled tender honeycomb
  tripe: 450 g/ 1 lb
- Black olives:
  100 g/ 4 oz/ ¼ cup
- 1 small red onion
- Parsley
- Olive oil
- Salt
- Pepper in a grinder

- Slice the tripe into thin strips, then season with the finely chopped onion, the stoned olives, the chopped parsley and the salt.
- Sprinkle with good olive oil, stir well and sprinkle with freshly ground pepper. Keep in a cool place before serving.

This simple starter is really delicious. The ingredients can vary; for example, you can add pickles, cooked ham in strips or a little mustard. According to taste, you can also add a few drops of lemon juice.

Panzanella
Bread and vegetable salad

Ingredients for 6 people

- Whole-wheat bread:
  600 g/ 1¼ lb
- 6 ripe salad tomatoes
- 3 red onions
- 2 cucumbers
- Basil
- Extra virgin olive oil
- Red vinegar
- Salt

- Thickly slice the bread (which should be 2 or 3 days old) and soak it for about a quarter of an hour in cold water.
- When softened, take a little at a time, press it and then squeeze it well between your hands; the crumbs, although quite dry, should remain whole.
- Place the bread in a large salad bowl (preferably wooden), add salt and all the vegetables, finely sliced, and the basil leaves.

- Flavour with salt and sprinkle with very good olive oil, toss well and place in the fridge.
- Before serving, add some vinegar, mix well and if desired, garnish with extra sliced tomatoes, onions and basil leaves.

Panzanella is a quick and simple dish, created by farm workers to use up their stale bread.

The typical bread should be cooked in a fire oven. The vegetables must be extremely fresh; the onions red and the oil and vinegar, genuine and full of flavour.

As far as the vegetables are concerned, different varieties can be added: lettuce, chicory, radishes, celery, parsley and even anchovy fillets.

Let me say that this is a dish which permits many variations, even if tradition suggests the above vegetables.

In Florence, cucumbers are used, but some people do not like them. In this case, replace them with pieces of celery stalk.

Polpettine della nonna
Grandma's fried meatballs

Ingredients for 4 people

- Left-over boiled beef: 300g/ 11 oz
- 2 boiled potatoes
- 2 eggs
- 1 garlic clove
- 3 tablespoons grated Parmesan
- Parsley
- Plain flour
- A little milk
- Nutmeg
- Salt and pepper
- Oil for frying

- Place the beef on a chopping board and with a heavy, sharp knife chop it very finely.
- Place the chopped meat in a bowl together with the eggs, puréed potatoes, Parmesan, garlic, parsley, a touch of nutmeg, salt and pepper.
- Mix the ingredients with a little milk, then make long, thin patties.
- Roll them in the flour and fry in plenty of hot oil.

These are the traditional meatballs made in every family to use up left-over meat. Today they make a delicious starter and are served in many restaurants.

Porrata
Leek tart

Ingredients for 6 people

- Leeks: 900 g/ 2 lb
- Plain flour:
  300 g/ 11 oz/ 3 cups
- Cake yeast:
  20 g/ ¾ oz/ 1 cake
- 3 eggs
- "Pancetta" or bacon:
  100 g/ 3 oz
- Olive oil
- Salt and pepper

- Heap up the flour and make a well. In this place the yeast (dissolved in 6 tablespoons of warm water), one egg, 4 tablespoons of oil and a little salt.
- Knead the dough well, make a ball and leave it to rest in a warm place for about one hour.
- In the meantime, clean the leeks by removing the root and the outer leaves, then wash and cut in thin slices up to the point where the white turns to pale green.
- Place the sliced leeks in a saucepan with 4 tablespoons of oil. Salt, cover and cook over a moderate heat until soft. Leave to cool and then mix in 2 eggs and a little pepper.
- Grease a baking pan (25 cm/ 10 inch diameter) with butter and line the bottom and sides with the dough, in this lay the sliced bacon and cover with the leeks.
- Cook in a moderate oven (190°C/ 375°F/ 5) for about half an hour.

This leek pie is my own interpretation of the fourteenth century "porréa". This was such a popular dish that it gave its name to a religious function, the "Uffizio della porrea", and to a feast, which took place in front of the "Basilica of San Lorenzo" in the month of August on the Saint's day.

In those days, this dish was certainly not considered a starter, but today it makes a tasty appetiser, if served hot and in small portions.

The word "porrèa" is the root of the word "purée".

Salvia fritta
Sage fritters

Ingredients

- Large fresh sage leaves
- Anchovies in oil
- 2 eggs
- Plain flour
- Salt
- Oil for frying

- Choose large, juicy, scented leaves of sage.
- Rinse quickly in cold water and lay out on a dishcloth to dry.
- Dip these into the egg, beaten with a pinch of salt, then place a piece of anchovy between two leaves, held together with a wooden toothpick and, still dripping with the egg, dredge in the flour and place immediately in the hot oil.
- Fry for a few seconds and serve piping hot.

Fried sage is delicious and can also be prepared without the anchovies. Just dip the leaves into the egg and then into the flour or simply use a frying batter.

Torta di carciofi
Artichoke pie

Ingredients for 6 people

- Shortcrust pastry:
  300 g/ 11 oz
- 5 artichokes
- Butter: 60 g/ 2 oz / ¼ cup
- Plain flour:
  30 g/ 1 oz/ ¼ cup
- Milk: 500 cc/ 1 pint/

- 2 cups
- 2 tablespoons grated
  Parmesan
- 1 egg
- Olive oil
- Salt and pepper

- Clean the artichokes by removing the stalks and the tough outer leaves and choke, then slice finely.
- Sauté in a pan with about 1 tablespoon of butter and 2 tablespoons of olive oil, salt and pepper, then add a couple of tablespoons of water to make them tender.
- In the meantime, prepare a béchamel sauce with the milk, flour, 2 tablespoons of butter, salt, pepper and Parmesan.
- Butter a tart tin (about 23 cm/ 9 inches diameter) and line with a very thin disc obtained from half of the pastry. Place the artichokes on this and cover with the béchamel sauce.
- Cover the whole dish with another disc of pastry, stick the two parts together well and brush the surface with a beaten egg.
- Cook in a moderate oven (180°C/ 350°F/ 4) for about half an hour.

Pastry for savoury pies and tarts

Instead of shortcrust pastry (long and difficult to prepare, but nowadays available frozen), I would suggest this pastry recipe, which is useful for all savoury dishes.

On a table, mix together 300 g/ 11 oz/ 2¼ cups of flour with 100 g/ 3 oz / ¼ cup of butter, 4 tablespoons of oil, 2 egg yolks, 1 whole egg, salt and half a cup of water.

Knead together well, but not for too long. Make a ball, cover and leave to stand in a cool place for at least one hour.

Roll it out with a rolling pin and flour or even spread the dough directly into the baking pan with your fingers.

Torta di fegatini
Chicken liver pie

Ingredients for 6 people

- Chicken livers:
  450 g/ 1 lb
- Cooked ham: 100 g/ 3 oz
- Grated Parmesan:
  30 g/ 1 oz/ ¼ cup
- 3 eggs
- Plain flour: 2 tablespoons

- Butter
- White wine
- Nutmeg
- Cinnamon
- Olive oil
- Salt and pepper

- Sauté the chicken livers in 2 tablespoons of butter and 3 tablespoons of oil, baste with a little wine and bring to the boil.
- Remove from the heat and chop the livers finely with the ham (you can also use a food processor with blades), then place the mixture in a bowl.
- Add the Parmesan, the eggs, the spices, the flour, a little oil, salt and pepper, mix well and transfer into a buttered and floured baking pan.
- Cook in a moderate oven (190°C/ 375°F/ 5) for about half an hour.
- Serve warm with toasted bread and pickles.

This fourteenth century recipe can also be made into a tart, using the pastry described above.

Salse
e Sughi
Sauces

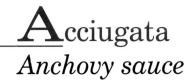

Acciugata
Anchovy sauce

Ingredients for 4 people

- 4 large salted anchovies
- 1 garlic clove
- 1 tablespoon capers

- Parsley
- Olive oil
- Salt and pepper

- Wash, rinse and remove all the bones from the anchovies.
- In a casserole (preferably earthenware), sauté the garlic clove in 5 spoonfuls of oil.
- Before it begins to colour, add the anchovies and help them to dissolve using a wooden spoon.
- Remove the garlic and add the finely chopped parsley and capers, salt and pepper to taste, then stir well and remove from heat.

This sauce is excellent with pasta, boiled beans, meat and poultry.

An antique sauce

The Greeks, but above all the Romans, were very keen on "garum", a sauce very similar to the anchovy sauce described above.

"Allec" was also very common; it was a smelly mixture made with the entrails of salted anchovies.

In the old times, anchovies were mainly eaten salted (it seems that the word "anchovy" actually means "salted"). As a matter of fact salt was so expensive that it was used as a form of currency (the origin of the word "salary" is the Latin for salt).

Thus the anchovies not only flavoured but also salted Roman food.

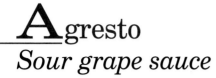Agresto
Sour grape sauce

Ingredients for 4 people

- Sour grapes: 300 g/ 11 oz
- 6 walnuts
- A handful of the soft part of the bread
- A bunch of parsley
- ½ onion
- 1 garlic clove
- 1 tablespoon sugar
- Olive oil
- Salt and pepper

- Shell the nuts and place them in a mortar together with the grapes, the finely chopped onion, the parsley, the garlic, the sugar and the bread; mix these ingredients together and then strain through a sieve (you can use a food processor with excellent results).
- Place this creamy mixture into a casserole, add 2 spoonfuls of oil, salt, pepper and heat without reaching boiling point. If too thick, dilute with a little broth or vinegar.
- This sauce should be preserved in jars under oil.
- It is good with boiled and roast meat or poultry.

"Agresto" is the juice made from unripe grapes, still green and sour. It was once used in place of lemon and vinegar.

Popular tradition endowed this sauce with great powers: it was an aphrodisiac, a pain killer, a disinfectant and helped mothers-to-be in giving birth.

Traditionally the agresto sauce was prepared at the beginning of the summer when the grapes were not yet mature and the walnuts fresh. If you wish to make it in winter, you can substitute the grape juice with lemon or vinegar but the taste will be completely different.

Crespelle alla fiorentina

Minestra di trippa e riso

Besciamella
Béchamel sauce

Ingredients

- Milk: ½ litre/ 1 pint/ 2 cups
- Plain flour: 3 tablespoons
- Butter: 4 tablespoons
- Nutmeg
- Salt and pepper

- Melt the butter in a saucepan, then add the flour and, stirring all the time, allow the mixture to cook slightly.
- Add a little salt, pepper and grated nutmeg, then stirring constantly, add the boiling hot milk little by little.
- Cook over a low heat for about 5 minutes, stirring all the time, until the sauce is thick and smooth

These are the ingredients for a béchamel sauce of medium consistency. For some dishes, if you need this to be more liquid, reduce the quantity of flour and butter and increase that of the milk.

Béchamel sauce is made with milk when accompanying vegetables or pasta dishes, whereas it is made with meat broth, if served with meats, or fish broth, if served with fish.

Is Béchamel sauce a Florentine invention?

Apart from a few exceptions, béchamel sauce does not appear in traditional Florentine dishes; and yet this antique sauce has a right to a place in this book.

This is how the story goes:

Béchamel sauce is perhaps not Florentine, but neither is it French as its name would suggest.

The butler of Louis XIV (the Sun King), the Marquis Louis de Béchamel, gave his name (at the beginning of the eighteenth century) to a sauce already described in Italian Renaissance cookbooks. Furthermore, in the "Libro della cucina del XIV secolo" by an anonymous Tuscan writer, a certain "biancomangiare" (white food) is mentioned, its preparation being identical to that of the famous béchamel.

Even Catherine Medici is said to have taught her French cooks how to prepare a "glue" to hold together the popular "mangiari bianchi" (white foods).

Not only béchamel, but other Italian sauces ("savori" as they were called then) of the Mediaeval and Renaissance periods were adopted by the French people and contributed to the success of that sophisticated cuisine.

Mostarda del Chianti
"Chianti" mustard

Ingredients

- Black or white grapes: 2 Kg/ 4 lb
- Red apples: 1 Kg/ 2 lb
- Pears: 500 g/ 1 lb
- Candied orange peels: 50 g/ 1¾ oz
- Mustard powder: 50 g/ 1¾
- Candied citron-rind: 50 g/ 1¾ oz
- 2 tablespoons honey
- 2 cups white wine
- Red vinegar
- Salt

- Press the grapes well and strain the juice.
- Place the peeled and sliced apples and pears into a saucepan, together with the white wine.
- Slowly cook until the wine has evaporated, then add the grape juice, honey, a pinch of salt and heat until the mixture has the consistency of jam.
- Remove from the heat and add the candied fruit in little pieces, the mustard and a cup of excellent vinegar. Stir well and when the mixture is cold, place in glass preserving jars.
- It is delicious with boiled and roast meat or poultry.

The word mustard comes from the Latin "mustum" (must). This is a traditional recipe made in the wonderful area between Florence and Siena called Chianti (pron.: keeantee), world famous for its red wines.

This dish, already described in the fourteenth century, is no longer prepared but I would really suggest trying it.

Salsa di noci
Walnut sauce

Ingredients

- Walnuts: 1 Kg/ 2 lb (unshelled)
- Parsley
- 1 tablespoon capers
- White vinegar
- Olive oil
- Salt and pepper

- Shell the nuts and crush them well in a mortar with a handful of parsley leaves and the capers (you can use a food processor with blades).
- Strain this mixture through a sieve and add a little oil gradually, stirring all the time as though making mayonnaise.
- When this is quite thick, salt, pepper and add a tablespoon of vinegar, stirring all the time.
- This sauce is excellent with boiled and roast meat and poultry.

This traditional Florentine sauce is usually prepared in the summer, when the walnuts are fresh. In other months, it can be prepared with dried nuts and a little vinegar or lemon juice; the sauce will be just as tasty.
If you do not own a mortar, you may use a food processor.

Salsa di peperoni
Sweet pepper sauce

Ingredients

- 2 sweet red peppers
- 1 garlic clove
- A handful of the soft part of the bread
- Vinegar
- Olive oil
- Salt and pepper

- Slice open the peppers and remove the seeds, then roast slightly in the oven or grill.
- Peel them and crush in the mortar together with the garlic and a handful of soft bread soaked in vinegar (you may use the food processor)
- Put the mixture in a saucepan, salt, pepper and add oil, stirring constantly.
- This sauce is served with boiled meat, poultry and fish.

There is another version of this sauce, also extremely good: it is called "salsa rossa" (red sauce). The peppers are crushed together with two ripe seedless tomatoes, the mixture is cooked for ten minutes.
Allow to cool and then add the oil.

Salsa di pinoli
Pine nut sauce

Ingredients

- Shelled pine nuts:
  100 g/ 3½ oz/ ¾ cup
- 2 salted anchovy fillets
- A handful of the soft part
  of the bread
- 1 teaspoon sugar
- ½ lemon
- Vinegar
- Olive oil
- Salt and pepper

- Crush the pine nuts in a mortar together with the cleaned anchovy fillets, the sugar, a pinch of salt and pepper and the bread soaked in vinegar.
- Strain this through a sieve and slowly pour a little olive oil into this purée stirring constantly (you can use the food processor for this).
- When the mixture is creamy, add a little lemon juice.

This sauce is served with boiled meat or poultry.

Salsa di pomodoro
Tomato sauce

Ingredients

- Ripe plum tomatoes:
  1 Kg/ 2 lb
- 2 medium carrots
- 1 stalk celery
- 1 onion
- 5 basil leaves
- 1 sprig parsley
- Olive oil
- Salt

- In a large saucepan, place 6 spoonfuls of oil, the crushed tomatoes and the other vegetables and herbs, all finely sliced apart from the basil and the parsley, which can be roughly cut with a pair of scissors.
- Salt and cook uncovered over a moderate heat for about one hour, leave to cool and strain.
- Return this sauce to the heat and reduce until the right consistency has been obtained.

If fresh tomatoes are not available, you can use canned Italian plum tomatoes.

This tomato sauce is so good that I would suggest you prepare some for the winter. In this case, cook at least 5 Kg / 10 lb of tomatoes and increase accordingly the herbs and vegetables.

Since it must last a long time, cook it for longer (about two hours before straining, and another two after).

Pour into sterilised dark glass bottles, cover with a thin layer of oil and cap.

Salsa peposa
Peppery sauce

Ingredients for 4 people

- Chicken livers: 150 g/ 5 oz
- ½ cup white wine
- A handful of the soft part of the bread
- 3 juniper berries
- A little broth
- ½ garlic clove
- 2 sage leaves
- Nutmeg
- Olive oil
- Salt and pepper

- Sauté the chicken livers in 6 spoonfuls of oil with the garlic and sage, then chop finely and strain.
- Place the purée in a casserole and add the bread soaked in vinegar, the wine and a ladleful of broth.
- Add the crushed berries, a pinch of nutmeg, salt and lots of pepper, as the name of the recipe suggests (you can use the food processor).
- Boil for a couple of minutes until the sauce is creamy.

This "peposa" sauce has been used since ancient times and is excellent served with roast guinea-fowl, turkey, chicken or game.

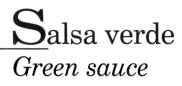Salsa verde
Green sauce

Ingredients for 4 people

- A large bunch of parsley
- 1 egg
- 2 anchovy fillets in oil
- 1 tablespoon capers in vinegar
- 2 tablespoons pine nuts
- 2 tablespoons mixed pickles
- ½ garlic clove
- Olive oil
- Salt and pepper

- Hard boil the egg, then chop with a knife on a board, together with all the other ingredients.
- You should obtain a fine mixture and, if possible, pound to a paste in a marble mortar (the food processor also provides excellent results).
- Place in a bowl, salt, pepper lightly and dilute, stirring constantly, with good olive oil until the sauce is creamy.
- Wait for a few minutes before serving.

This sauce is perfect with boiled meat. It can also be prepared substituting the egg with either bread soaked in vinegar and then squeezed, or a slice of boiled potato. The pine nuts are optional.

In Florence "salsa verde" has always been a favourite; once there were even street sellers of this sauce. They usually came from the countryside; they collected fresh and scented herbs and knew how to mix them well.

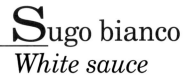Sugo bianco
White sauce

Ingredients for 4 people

- Rabbit meat: 100 g/ 3½ oz
- Chicken breast: 100 g/ 3½ oz
- Sweetbreads: 100 g/ 3½ oz
- 1 small onion
- 1 small carrot
- Rosemary
- White wine
- A little broth
- Olive oil
- Salt and pepper

- S...
bay...
- B...
into
- Af...
add...
- Sa...

- Chop the onion, carrot and a few leaves of rosemary, then sauté in a pan with 6 spoonfuls of olive oil. When the onion begins to soften, add the rabbit and chicken in pieces.
- Cook for a little, then add half a cup of white wine. Wait for this to evaporate, remove the meat from the heat and roughly chop on the chopping board. Return to the pan and add the cleaned, boiled sweetbreads, cut into cubes.
- Salt and pepper, then continue cooking whilst adding the broth. The final mixture should be smooth and creamy.

This sauce is a perfect accompaniment to home-made noodles.

Su...

Simp...

Sugo dell'ortolano

Greengrocer's sauce

Ingre...

- Rip...
  tom...
- 1 or...
- 2 ca...
- 2 st...

- Ch...
- Wh...
a low
- Ad...
anoth

Th...
sauce
real t...
Ho...

Ingredients for 4 people

- Fresh ripe (or canned) tomatoes: 500 g / 1 lb
- 1 artichoke
- 2 courgettes (zucchini)
- 1 stalk celery
- 1 carrot

- ½ onion
- 1 sprig parsley
- Chilli pepper
- Olive oil
- Salt

- Chop the onion, parsley and a little chilli pepper and then sauté in about 4 spoonfuls of oil.
- Shortly after, add all the other vegetables (except the tomatoes) cut into thin slices. Salt and leave to flavour for ten minutes.
- Add the sliced tomatoes and cook over a low heat for about half an hour or until the carrot is completely cooked. If the mixture becomes too dry, add a little broth.

This is a truly delicious sauce. The vegetables can be chosen according to season and personal taste. I have experimented with aubergine (eggplant), fennel, cucumbers, radishes and it is always good.
If in season, do not forget to add some basil.

Cipollata
Onion and pork soup

Ingredients for 4 people

- 4 large white or golden onions
- 4 slices of whole-wheat bread
- 2 Italian pork sausages
- Pancetta (unsmoked bacon): 50 g/ 1¾ oz
- Pork spare ribs: 150 g/ 5 oz
- Broth: 1,2 litre/ 2 pints/ 5 cups
- Grated Parmesan
- Olive oil
- Salt and pepper

- In a pot sauté the sliced onions with 6 spoonfuls of oil for 10 minutes.
- Add the skinned and halved sausages and the spare ribs and the diced bacon.
- After 10 minutes add the boiling hot broth.
- Cook uncovered for about an hour, adding salt to taste and serve the soup on slices of toasted bread.
- Sprinkle with pepper and grated Parmesan.

The meat can be excluded, making this a simple, but tasty, onion soup.

Cavolo con le fette
Cabbage on toast

Ingredients for 4 people

- "Black" Tuscan cabbage (see note): 4 bunches
- 4 slices whole-wheat bread
- Garlic
- Extra virgin olive oil
- Salt
- Black pepper in a grinder

- Prepare and clean the cabbage, taking care to leave the bunches whole, then boil these for about one hour in a pot with boiling salted water (it is advisable to add a bouillon cube).
- In the meantime, slice four pieces of bread (each slice should include all

- Sauté the chopped onion and garlic in 4 spoonfuls of oil, add a couple of bay leaves.
- Before the onion begins to colour, add the sausage, skinned and broken into little pieces.
- After five minutes, add half a cup of red wine and when this has evaporated, add the tomatoes.
- Salt slightly, pepper and cook for about half an hour.

Sugo finto
Simple "false" tomato sauce

Ingredients for 4 people

- Ripe (or canned) plum tomatoes: 500 g/ 1 lb
- 1 onion
- 2 carrots
- 2 stalk celery
- 1 sprig parsley
- Basil (if in season)
- ½ cup red wine
- Olive oil
- Salt and pepper

- Chop the carrots, celery and onion very finely and sauté in 4 spoonfuls of oil.
- When the vegetables begin to soften, add the wine and leave to reduce over a low heat.
- Add the tomatoes in pieces and the basil; salt, pepper and leave to cook for another half an hour.

This delicious sauce is called "false" in Italian because it is similar to a meat sauce, but without the meat. It is similar to tomato sauce but yet it is not a real tomato sauce.

However, it is traditional, quick and tasty.

Sugo ricco
Rich sauce

Ingredients for 4 people

- Ground (minced) beef: 200 g/ 7 oz
- Chicken breast: 100 g/ 3½
- Chicken livers: 50 g/ 1¾ oz
- Bacon: 50 g/ 1¾ oz
- Ripe (or canned) plum tomatoes: 500 g/ 1 lb

- 1 onion
- 1 carrot
- 1 stalk celery
- ½ cup wine
- Olive oil
- Salt and pepper

- Sauté in a casserole the finely chopped onion, carrot and celery in 6 spoonfuls of oil, together with little pieces of bacon.
- When the onion begins to turn transparent, add the meat, the chopped chicken breast (in not too small pieces), the finely chopped chicken livers and leave to sauté for 10 minutes, then pour in the wine (either red or white).
- When this has evaporated, add the tomatoes; salt, pepper and leave to cook for one hour.
- The sauce should be quite thick.

This is the exact opposite of the "Sugo finto"; here there is lots of meat! It is a rich sauce for special occasions and is excellent with pasta.

Minestre
e Zuppe
Soups
and Pulses

Brodo appollocato
Chicken broth

Ingredients for 4 people

- Assorted pieces of beef:
  500 g/ 1 lb
- ½ chicken
- A couple of bones
  (shin, marrow)

- 1 onion
- 2 carrots
- 1 stalk celery
  with its leaves
- Coarse salt

- Put all ingredients in a large stockpot: the beef cut into large pieces, the chicken into quarters, the bones and the cleaned and sliced carrots, celery and onion.
- Add about 2 litres/ 3½ pints/ 8 cups of water, salt, cover and simmer very slowly for at least 2 hours.
- Remove the chicken when overcooked and it starts to break up.
- When cooked, strain through a fine sieve.
- To eliminate the fat, leave in the fridge. The broth will form a crust of fat which can be easily removed.

This is the traditional recipe for an excellent broth, known as "appollocato", since it includes "pollo" (chicken), but it can also be prepared with just the beef.

For a perfect result, use at least two or three types of meat (flank, brisket, shin, neck).

Brodo del parto
Confinement broth

Ingredients for 4 people

- T-bone steak: about 700 g/ 1½ lb
- ½ small onion
- 1 stalk celery
- 1 carrot
- 1 sprig parsley
- 1 nut butter
- ½ glass vintage red Chianti wine
- Salt

- Sauté in an earthenware casserole the very finely chopped onion in the butter and when this begins to colour, add the steak cut into pieces, and its bone. Allow the meat to brown over a high heat.
- At this point add the celery and the carrot, 1 litre/ 1¾ pint/ 4 cups of cold water and the salt.
- Cook very slowly for about three hours until the liquid has reduced to not more than four small teacups of broth.
- Remove the meat and filter the broth. Serve hot in a cup with a dash of Chianti reserve wine.

This is an exceptional broth (in every sense, including cost); a sort of cordial traditionally given to women who had just given birth. I would however advise anyone (even if you have not just given birth) to try this wonderful consommé.

In an anonymous manuscript from 1200, kept in the Biblioteca Laurenziana, one reads that:

"When confined women and the ill are weak and are disgusted by vegetarian food, yet wish to eat meat, we must satisfy their natural desires.

One should be careful not to give them fatty meat because the fat might cause the fever to return.

If the patient is unable to swallow, because of a dry and inflamed throat, they need to be given a good meat broth which is both food and drink.

This will soothe their throat like an unguent."

Finally, two recommendations: do not substitute the steak with any other meat and always use an excellent dark red Chianti, at least 6 to 8 years old.

Carabaccia
Onion soup

Ingredients for 4 people

- 4 large onions
- 2 stalks celery
- 2 carrots
- Broth: 1 litre/ 1¾ pints/ 4 cups

- Whole-wheat bread
- Grated Parmesan
- Olive oil
- Salt and pepper

- Clean and cut the onions, celery and carrots into small cubes.
- Place these in an earthenware casserole together with 6 spoonfuls of oil, then salt, pepper and cover.
- Cook slowly for about half an hour. Stir often but do not add any water: the vegetables themselves will provide plenty.
- Add the broth, then continue to simmer slowly for another half an hour.
- Toast 4 slices of bread and place one in each bowl. Cover with the "carabaccia" and sprinkle with grated parmesan.

When one talks of onion soup, the French "soupe à l'oignon" comes to mind, made famous throughout the world by the restaurants around "Les Halles" (the former markets of Paris).

However, the root of all modern onion soups can be considered the Florentine "carabaccia".

The above recipe is not the original Renaissance one. This would not be popular today as it included almonds, sugar and cinnamon!

The name "carabaccia" derives from the Greek "karabos", meaning "boat in the form of a nut shell". The word was used for the soup tureen and then for the soup itself.

Cipollata
Onion and pork soup

Ingredients for 4 people

- 4 large white or golden onions
- 4 slices of whole-wheat bread
- 2 Italian pork sausages
- Pancetta (unsmoked bacon): 50 g/ 1¾ oz
- Pork spare ribs: 150 g/ 5 oz
- Broth: 1,2 litre/ 2 pints/ 5 cups
- Grated Parmesan
- Olive oil
- Salt and pepper

- In a pot sauté the sliced onions with 6 spoonfuls of oil for 10 minutes.
- Add the skinned and halved sausages and the spare ribs and the diced bacon.
- After 10 minutes add the boiling hot broth.
- Cook uncovered for about an hour, adding salt to taste and serve the soup on slices of toasted bread.
- Sprinkle with pepper and grated Parmesan.

The meat can be excluded, making this a simple, but tasty, onion soup.

Cavolo con le fette
Cabbage on toast

Ingredients for 4 people

- "Black" Tuscan cabbage (see note): 4 bunches
- 4 slices whole-wheat bread
- Garlic
- Extra virgin olive oil
- Salt
- Black pepper in a grinder

- Prepare and clean the cabbage, taking care to leave the bunches whole, then boil these for about one hour in a pot with boiling salted water (it is advisable to add a bouillon cube).
- In the meantime, slice four pieces of bread (each slice should include all

Cavolo con le fette

Crema di porri

the crust), then toast well and rub one side with a garlic clove.
- Dip quickly in the cabbage water, then place on a serving dish or directly on individual dishes.
- Place a well cooked and drained cabbage bunch on each slice of bread.
- Salt slightly, add abundant oil and grind some fresh pepper on top. This is simply delicious!

The "black" Tuscan cabbage only grows at the first sign of cold weather, just when the olive oil, essential for this tasty dish, has been pressed.

Unfortunately it not possible to find this vegetable outside Italy, but you can try this recipe by replacing the black cabbage with Savoy cabbage leaves or other crinkly or curly green cabbage.

However, a top class Italian extra virgin olive oil is essential.

Crema di porri
Leek cream soup

Ingredients for 4 people

- 6 medium sized leeks
- Broth: 1 litre /1¾ pints / 4 cups
- 2 tablespoons plain flour
- Butter: 50 g /1¾ oz / ¼ cup
- Grated Parmesan
- Salt and pepper

- Clean and finely slice the leeks up to the pale green part of the stem. Place in a pot and sauté slowly in the butter.
- After a few minutes, sprinkle with flour and cook for five minutes. Add the boiling hot broth.
- Salt to taste and cook for a further 40 minutes; the soup should be creamy and smooth in consistency.
- Serve hot, with grated Parmesan, pepper and, if desired, with slices of bread fried in butter.

Leeks, already popular in Roman times, have always been a favourite in Florence.

In the fourteenth century, for the feast of San Lorenzo, there was a public ceremony in San Lorenzo square, during which the "porrèa" was served.

It is not exactly clear what this was: either a soup or a sort of savoury tart.

Nevertheless, it was from this dish that the word purée derives.

Minestra di fagioli
Bean soup

Ingredients for 4 people

- Short pasta or noodles:
  200 g/ 7 oz
- Fresh white (haricot)
  beans: 300 g/ 11 oz/ 3 cups
  (shelled)
- Ripe or canned tomatoes:
  100 g/ 3½ oz

- Pork lard: 50 g/ 1¾ oz
- 1 garlic clove
- A handful of parsley
- Chilli pepper
- Olive oil
- Salt and pepper

- Boil the beans in 1,2 litres/ 2 pints/ 5 cups of salted water, when they are cooked, strain through a sieve and put the creamed mixture back into the cooking water.
- In a pot, sauté the lard, chopped parsley, garlic clove and a little chilli pepper in 4 spoonfuls of oil. As soon as the garlic begins to colour add the tomatoes, salt and pepper and cook for a further ten minutes.
- Add all the bean liquid and cook for a further fifteen minutes. Finally, add the pasta and cook, making sure that the result is neither too liquid nor too thick.
- Serve with a little oil and preferably without Parmesan.

If you use dried beans they need soaking overnight

Minestra di fagioli con l'occhio
Black-eyed bean soup

Ingredients for 4 people

- Dried black-eyed beans:
  200 g/ 7 oz/ 2 cups
- Rice: 200 g/ 7 oz/ 1 cup
- ¼ Savoy cabbage
- 1 onion
- 1 carrot

- 1 stalk celery
- 1 garlic clove
- Sage
- Olive oil
- Salt and pepper

- Place the beans to soak overnight and then boil in 1,2 litres/ 2 pints/ 5 cups of salted water having added the sage and the garlic.
- When they are well cooked, strain half through the sieve and put the purée back in the cooking water;
- In another saucepan, sauté the finely chopped onion, carrot and celery in 5 spoonfuls of oil together with the cabbage cut into strips. After about ten minutes, add all the broth with the beans and bring to the boil, then add the rice.
- Salt, pepper, adjust the quantity of water and finish cooking the rice.
- Serve this soup hot with a little olive oil on top.

As it is well known, beans originate from America, so in the past, the Florentines had to prepare bean soups with the "black-eyed" variety from the tropical regions of Asia and Africa.
This bean, also called Egyptian or Chinese bean, was introduced to Italy from Greece.

Minestra di trippa e riso
Tripe and rice soup

Ingredients for 4 people

- Tripe: 450 g/ 1 lb
- Rice: 200 g/ 7 oz/ 1 cup
- Broth: 1,5 litres/ 2 pints/ 5 cups
- 1 onion
- 1 carrot
- 1 stalk celery
- 1 tablespoon tomato paste
- Grated Parmesan
- Olive oil
- Salt and pepper

- Finely chop the onion, celery and carrot and sauté in 4 spoonfuls of oil. When the onion begins to soften, add the tripe cut into strips.
- Salt, pepper and add the tomato paste dissolved in a little broth, and then pour in the rest of the broth.
- Bring to the boil, add the rice and cook, leaving the pot uncovered.
- Leave to stand for a little, then serve the soup hot with Parmesan.

This delicious soup can also be prepared adding about 300 g / 11 oz of Swiss chard, well cleaned and cut into strips.

Minestra di pane
Bread and bean soup

Ingredients for 4 people

- Fresh white (haricot) beans: 300 g/ 11 oz/ 1¼ cup (shelled)
- Ripe or canned tomatoes: 300 g/ 11 oz
- ½ Savoy cabbage
- 1 stalk celery
- 1 onion
- A handful of parsley
- 1 garlic clove
- Chilli pepper
- Whole-wheat bread
- Olive oil
- Salt and pepper

- In a fairly large saucepan, sauté the garlic, the finely chopped onion, celery, parsley and chilli in 6 spoonfuls of oil.
- Add the peeled, chopped tomatoes, salt and cook slowly for about 10 minutes.
- At this point, pour into the saucepan half of the already boiled beans and about 1,2 litres/ 2 pints/ 5 cups of the water in wich they have been cooked.
- Add the other half of the beans, having strained them through the sieve and the finely chopped Savoy cabbage.
- Cook slowly for about three quarters of an hour and serve, as usual, on sliced and toasted bread, lightly rubbed with garlic. Sprinkle with good extra virgin olive oil and no Parmesan cheese.

Minestra di patate
Potato soup

Ingredients for 4 people

- Potatoes: 700 g/ 1½ lb
- Ripe or canned tomatoes: 100 g/ 4 oz
- 1 onion
- 2 small carrots
- 1 stalk celery
- 1 sprig parsley
- Grated Parmesan
- Whole-wheat bread
- Olive oil
- Salt and pepper

- Peel the potatoes and cut them into large pieces, then place in a pot together with the celery, onion, carrots and tomatoes.
- Add 1½ litres/ 2½ pints/ 6 cups of water; salt, pepper and cook slowly for about three quarters of an hour.
- Take out the vegetables and strain through a sieve. Put back into the pot, add four spoonfuls of oil and cook for a further quarter of an hour (you can use a hand-held mixer).

This soup may be served with little cubes of bread fried in a little oil or with short pasta; in the latter case, leave the soup a little more liquid.
In both cases, serve with grated cheese.

Minestra di riso e fagioli
Rice and bean soup

Ingredients for 4 people

- Fresh white (haricot) beans: 300 g/ 11 oz/ 1¼ cups (shelled)
- Ripe or canned tomatoes: 200 g/ 7 oz
- Rice: 200 g/ 7 oz/ 1 cup
- 1 onion
- 1 garlic clove
- 1 stalk celery
- 1 sprig parsley
- Chilli pepper
- Olive oil
- Salt

- Cook the beans in 2 litres/ 3½ pints/ 8 cups or of cold salted water.
- In the meanwhile, sauté the finely chopped onion, celery, garlic and parsley in 4 spoonfuls of oil.
- When the onion begins to colour, add the chopped tomatoes and continue to cook over a low heat for about a quarter of an hour.
- When the beans are cooked, add this sauce; salt to taste and after a few minutes add the rice.
- Continue to cook, adding boiling water if necessary, but remember that the soup should be semi-liquid.
- Serve hot with a little olive oil.

If you use dried beans, soak them overnight.

Minestra d'agnello
Lamb soup

Ingredients for 4 people

- Ground lean lamb: 300 g/ 11 oz
- Home-made narrow noodles: 200 g/ 7 oz
- Ripe or canned tomatoes: 200 g/ 7 oz
- ½ onion
- 1 carrot

- 1 stalk celery
- 1 garlic clove
- ½ glass white wine
- Broth: 1 litre/ 1¾ pints/ 4 cups
- Olive oil
- Salt and pepper

- Finely chop the celery, carrot and onion and sauté in 3 spoonfuls of oil; as soon as the onion begins to colour, add the lamb and continue to cook.
- After a few minutes, add the wine and allow to evaporate completely, then add the tomatoes.
- Continue to cook over a low heat for about one hour, then add the broth.
- Finally add the noodles and cook for a few minutes. Serve with freshly ground pepper.

Minestrone
Florentine vegetable soup

Ingredients for 6 people

- Rice: 200 g/ 7 oz
- Fresh white (haricot) beans: 300 g/ 11 oz/ 1 cup (shelled or dried)
- Swiss chard: 300 g/ 10 oz
- 4 courgettes/zucchini
- 3 potatoes
- 4 Savoy cabbage leaves
- 2 onions

- 2 ripe (or canned) tomatoes
- 4 carrots
- 3 stalks celery
- 1 sprig parsley
- 1 bouillon cube
- Olive oil
- Salt and pepper

- In a large pot, sauté the finely chopped onion, celery and carrots in 6 spoonfuls of oil.
- When the onion begins to turn golden, add the other vegetables (rinsed but not dried), cut into slices, cubes or strips as you think best; add the bouillon cube and cook slowly, uncovered, without adding water.
- Stir frequently and when there is little liquid left, add boiling water. Salt and pepper to taste and, when the vegetables are cooked, add the rice with enough boiling water to allow this to cook. Simmer uncovered over a low heat.
- The "minestrone" is excellent served hot, lukewarm or even at room temperature; but always sprinke with good olive oil.

This "minestrone" can also be served with toasted slices of bread, rubbed with garlic, instead of the rice.

Pancotto
Bread soup

Ingredients for 4 people

- Stale bread: 250 g/ 9 oz
- 2 garlic cloves
- Grated Parmesan
- Olive oil
- Salt

- Boil about 1 litre/ 1¾ pints/ 4 cups of salted water in a pot, then add the thinly sliced bread and the peeled and crushed garlic cloves.
- Cook slowly for about a quarter of an hour, stirring constantly; then add 4 spoonfuls of oil and 4 of cheese.
- Cook for a few more minutes, then leave to cool slightly; serve with a little olive oil and more Parmesan.

In the past, a great deal of garlic was added to provide flavour; it was also good for the digestion and rid the intestines of worms.
"Pancotto" (literally "cooked bread") can rarely be found today, and yet is to be considered the ancestor of the famous "pappa al pomodoro" (tomato pap).
The "pappa" was in fact a sort of "pancotto", to which, from the beginning of the seventeenth century, tomatoes (imported from America) were added.

Pappa al pomodoro
Bread and tomato soup

Ingredients for 4 people

- Whole-wheat stale bread: 300 g/ 11 oz
- Ripe or canned plum tomatoes: 450 g/ 1 lb
- 1 medium sized leek
- Basil
- Chilli pepper
- Broth: 1 litre/ 1¾ pints/ 4 cups
- Olive oil
- Salt and pepper

- Sauté the finely sliced leek and chilli pepper in 6 spoonfuls of oil in a pot and when cooked, add chopped tomatoes and plenty of chopped fresh basil.
- Bring to the boil over a medium heat and five minutes later, add the broth.
- Salt and bring to the boil, add the thinly sliced bread. Leave to cook for a further ten minutes.
- Remove from heat and leave, covered, for about one hour. Before serving, stir well with a whisk.

The "pappa al pomodoro" can be eaten hot, lukewarm, at room temperature or reheated; but always sprinkle with olive oil, freshly ground pepper and, if you like, grated Parmesan.

This is one of the most famous Florentine dishes. It is served, in summer, in all restaurants.

Pasta e ceci
Pasta and chickpea soup

Ingredients for 4 people

- Dried chickpeas: 200 g/ 7 oz/ 1 cup
- Short pasta: 200 g/ 7 oz
- 1 garlic clove
- 1 sprig rosemary
- 2 ripe or canned tomatoes
- Olive oil
- Salt and pepper

- Soak the chickpeas overnight in cold water (with a spoonful of bicarbonate of soda) then, cook in about 1½ litres/ 2½ pints/ 6 cups of salted water.
- Add 3 spoonfuls of oil, the rosemary, the garlic and the chopped tomatoes.
- Simmer over a low heat for 2 hours.
- When the chick peas are well cooked, strain about a half through a sieve, then put the purée back into the pot and add the pasta.
- Finish cooking, pepper and salt to taste. The soup should be quite thick.
- Serve hot or lukewarm with some olive oil and preferably without cheese.

To abbreviate the cooking time, you can use canned chickpeas.

Pasta e fagioli
Pasta and bean soup

Ingredients for 4 people

- Ridged short pasta: 200 g/ 7 oz
- Dried white beans: 200 g/ 7 oz/ 1 cup
- 2 garlic cloves
- Rosemary
- Sage
- Chilli pepper
- Olive oil
- Salt and pepper

- Soak the beans overnight and boil them in the usual way with a garlic clove and some sage.
- Once they are well cooked, strain with all their liquid through a sieve in order to eliminate their skins. Put the creamy mixture back in the pot.
- Sauté the garlic clove, rosemary and chilli pepper in a pan then pour this oil over the beans, having removed the garlic first.
- Salt and pepper, bring to the boil and add the pasta and a little water, if necessary.
- Serve in an earthenware bowl, with a little olive oil and no cheese.

Two or three peeled plum tomatoes can also be added to this soup.

Ribollita
Bread and vegetable soup

Ingredients for 6 people

- Dried white beans:
  400 g/ 14 oz/ 2 cups
- ½ Savoy cabbage
- Swiss chard: 450 g/ 1 lb
- 3 ripe or canned
  tomatoes
- 2 stalks celery

- 2 carrots
- 1 onion
- 1 leek
- 2 garlic cloves
- 1 sprig thyme
- Whole-wheat bread
- Olive oil
- Salt and pepper

- Cook the beans (soaked overnight), retaining all the cooking water; take about three quarters and strain through a sieve straight back into their water. Keep aside the rest of the beans.
- In a large pot, sauté the finely chopped onion together with a clove of garlic in 8 tablespoons of oil. When these are golden, add the sliced celery, carrot and leek.
- Sauté for a while and then add the chopped tomatoes, the rinsed and sliced Swiss chard, Savoy cabbage, the thyme, salt and pepper.
- Pour in all the liquid from the beans and cook the soup very slowly for an hour, adding, if necessary, a little warm water. Towards the end, add the beans.
- Place slices of bread in the bottom of the bowl, pour over half the soup, cover with another layer of bread and then the rest of the soup.
- Before serving, leave to stand for a few minutes.
- Serve with a trickle of good extra virgin olive oil and no cheese.

Since this is a "spontaneous" dish, there are many versions and above all, the quantities of the ingredients are very variable. These reflect what is available at the moment of cooking and personal taste.

However, some versions of ribollita, red with tomatoes, oily and with only a few vegetables, are really not acceptable.

The traditional "ribollita" should really be re-boiled, in other words, re-cooked with some extra oil. But read the following note about this.

The very famous ribollita, pride of many a Florentine trattoria, cannot be considered a recipe in itself. In its original version, it was nothing but a poor and simple soup made with left-overs and boiled up the next day.

On Fridays, in the countryside, soup was prepared with the simplest of ingredients: bread, potatoes, cabbage, beans etc. and since a large quantity was made, it was re-heated the day after and eaten for breakfast!

Many versions of ribollita served today are nothing like this. They are excellent vegetable soups but have rarely been re-boiled.

If you wish to make a traditional ribollita, proceed like this: place the soup in a flameproof tureen, cover the surface with thin slices of onion, grind a little black pepper and sprinkle with very good olive oil; place in the oven and gratin until the onion is slightly golden. Serve hot without cheese.

Zuppa di baccalà
Salt cod soup

Ingredients for 4 people

- Salt cod (already soaked in water): 400 g/ 14 oz
- Broth: 1,2 litres/ 2 pints/ 5 cups
- Ripe or canned tomatoes: 300 g/ 11 oz
- 2 potatoes

- ½ onion
- 1 carrot
- 1 stalk celery
- Whole-wheat bread
- Olive oil
- Salt and pepper

- Skin and scale the soaked cod, then chop into small pieces.
- Sauté the finely chopped onion, carrot and celery in 5 tablespoons of oil; as soon as the onion begins to soften, add the cod and cook for a few minutes.
- Add the tomatoes and the pepper, cook for ten minutes before adding the boiling hot broth (prepared with bouillon cubes); add the peeled and cubed potatoes, salt then cook for about three quarters of an hour.
- Place a slice of toasted bread (rubbed with garlic, if desired) in each bowl and pour the soup over the top.

Zuppa di cavolo
Savoy cabbage soup

Ingredients for 4 people

- ½ Savoy cabbage
- Dried red (kidney) beans: 80 g/ 3 oz/ 1 cup
- 1 potato
- 2 ripe or canned tomatoes
- 1 stalk celery

- 1 onion
- 1 carrot
- 1 sprig thyme
- Whole-wheat bread
- Olive oil
- Salt and pepper

- Sauté the finely chopped onion, carrot and celery in 4 tablespoons of oil in a large pot. After a few minutes, add the tomatoes, the thyme and the peeled, roughly chopped, potato.
- Stir over the heat, then, little by little, add the washed and sliced cabbage leaves, the beans (soaked overnight) and 2 litres/ 3½ pints of cold water.
- Salt to taste, cover and cook for about 2 hours.
- Served with a slice of bread, sprinkle with extra virgin olive oil and no cheese.

Zuppa di cipolle e maiale
Pork and onion soup

Ingredients for 4 people

- Onions: 1 Kg/ 2¼ lb
- Pork spare ribs: 300 g/ 11 oz
- Bacon: 50 g/ 2 oz
- 1 Italian sausage
- 1 stalk celery

- 1 carrot
- 1 garlic clove
- Whole-wheat bread
- Olive oil
- Salt

- In a large pot boil the pork ribs, the carrot, the celery and half of the onion in 1½ litres/ 2½ pints of salted water.
- When the pork is cooked and comes away easily off the bone, remove from

the pot, bone and cut into thin slices.
- Slice the onion finely and sauté in a pot with 8 tablespoons of oil, the sliced bacon and the peeled sausage, broken into small pieces.
- Leave to sauté uncovered, then, a little at a time, add ladlefuls of broth.
- Cook for about 1 hour, add the pork and continue to cook for another half an hour.
- Serve on toasted slices of bread, rubbed with garlic, placed directly into the soup bowls.

Zuppa di porri
Leek soup

Ingredients for 4 people

- 5 leeks
- Gruyere cheese: 80 g/ 3 oz
- Butter: 50 g/ 1¾ oz/ ¼ cup
- 2 tablespoons flour
- Broth: 1,2 litres/ 2 pints/ 5 cups
- Whole-wheat bread
- Grated parmesan
- Salt and pepper in a grinder

- In a large pot sauté the cleaned and very finely sliced leeks (only the white part) in butter; sprinkle with the flour and, after ten minutes, add the broth. Leave to cook over a moderate heat for about half an hour.
- In the meantime, toast the bread in the oven; place two pieces in each bowl and sprinkle with grated gruyere cheese.
- When the soup is cooked, pour into each bowl, sprinkle with freshly ground black pepper and plenty of grated parmesan.

This excellent leek soup can be transformed into a delicious "minestrone", if, instead of the bread, you add 200 g/ 7 oz of rice.
For a richer soup, add sliced boiled chicken breast. In this case, there is no need for bread or rice.

Zuppa di trippa e zampa
Tripe and calf's foot soup

Ingredients for 4 people

- Tripe: 300 g/ 11 oz
- 1 calf's foot
- Broth: 1 litre/ 1¾ pints/ 4 cups
- Ripe or canned tomatoes: 300 g/ 11 oz
- 1 onion
- Whole-wheat bread
- Grated parmesan
- Olive oil
- Salt and pepper

- Boil the tripe and foot in a pot for about one hour; leave to cool then cut the tripe and the boned flesh from the foot into thin strips.
- Sauté the finely chopped onion in 4 tablespoons of oil; as soon as this begins to soften, add the meat, a pinch of salt and pepper. Cook for a quarter of an hour.
- Add the tomatoes and broth, cook for a further half of an hour.
- Place a slice of toasted bread in each soup bowl and pour the soup over the top; serve with Parmesan and freshly ground pepper.

If calf's foot is not available, you can use pig's trotter.

Zuppa frantoiana
Olive press soup

Ingredients for 6 people

- Freshly pressed extra virgin olive oil
- Dried red (kidney) beans: 300 g/ 11 oz / 3 cups
- ½ Savoy cabbage
- Swiss chard: 200 g/ 7 oz
- 3 potatoes
- 3 courgettes/zucchini
- 3 carrots
- 1 onion
- 1 stalk celery
- Garlic
- Salt and pepper
- Whole-wheat bread

- Boil the (soaked overnight) beans and strain through a sieve, leaving about 3 tablespoons whole.
- In a large pot, sauté the finely chopped onion, celery and carrot in 8 tablespoons of oil; after a little, add the puréed beans and their water.
- As soon as this boils, add all the other finely chopped vegetables, and the sliced carrots and courgettes.
- Cook for about three quarters of an hour (add water, if necessary), remembering that the soup should not be too thick. Before removing from the heat, add the whole beans.
- Thinly slice and toast the bread, rub with a little garlic.
- Place several slices in the bottom of the soup bowl and sprinkle with olive oil; pour half of the warm soup onto these, then cover with more bread slices, more oil, more soup and more oil.

In spite of the variety of ingredients, the olive press soup, as its name suggests, is essentially based on the oil, which should be abundant, freshly pressed and virgin; in other words, straight from the press!

This is why I have placed the oil at the top of the list of ingredients: it is the most important.

Another essential component are the beans which, with their taste and black appearance, are quite irreplaceable.

As far as the other flavourings and vegetables are concerned, these can be varied according to season and taste.

Zuppa lombarda
Bean soup

Ingredients for 4 people

- Fresh white (haricot) beans: 400 g/ 14 oz/ 4 cups (shelled)
- 2 garlic cloves
- 1 sprig sage
- Whole-wheat bread
- Olive oil
- Salt and pepper

- Cook the beans in 1,2 litres/ 2 pints/ 5 cups of cold salted water, add the garlic cloves, sage and 4 tablespoons of olive oil.
- Place a slice of lightly toasted bread in each bowl and cover with a ladleful of the boiling hot beans and broth.
- Salt and sprinkle with freshly ground pepper and good olive oil.

This simple yet delicious dish has a very strange name: it is completely unknown in Lombardy (a region in the North of Italy), but in Tuscany it is a traditional recipe: probably dating back to the beginning of the nineteenth century.

Perhaps this bean soup was particularly popular with the Lombards living in the Tuscan area.

It is also known as "bastard soup".

You can use dried beans (300 g/ 11 oz) soaked overnight.

Zuppa lombarda

Pappa al pomodoro

Pasta
e riso
Pasta
and Rice

Agnellotti
Meat stuffed pasta

Ingredients for 6 people

- Lean veal: 200 g/ 7 oz
- Veal brains: 100 g/ 3½ oz
- Boiled Swiss chard: 100 g/ 3½ oz
- Ricotta: 50 g/ 1¾ oz
- Soft part of bread: 50 g/ 1¾ oz
- 1 egg
- Butter: 100 g/ 3½ oz/ ½ cup
- Nutmeg
- Salt and pepper
- Pasta dough (400 g/ 12 oz/ 3 cups flour and 3 eggs)

- Firstly, prepare the pasta dough, kneading together the flour, the eggs, a little water and some salt. Make a ball and leave to rest in a plastic wrap for about one hour.
- Sauté the veal in the butter in a casserole, then add the boiled brains, the Swiss chard and the soft bread.
- Leave to cook for a little, then chop the mixture finely, place in a bowl together with the ricotta, the egg, a pinch of nutmeg, salt and pepper. Stir well until the mixture is smooth and even.
- Roll out the dough into a very thin sheet (with the rolling pin or the pasta machine), then place a teaspoon of the mixture every 8 cm/ 3 inches in a line. Cover with pastry.
- Cut out rounds with a glass or stencil about 7 cm/ 2½ inches in diameter, press delicately around the edge and seal with a fork (the agnellotti can be round, crescent shaped, or even rectangular).
- Leave to stand well apart on a floured tea towel, then cook in broth or salted water for a few minutes.
- Remove from the water with a perforated spoon (if possible do no use a colander) and serve with a good meat sauce or butter and Parmesan.

If you wish to taste the real "agnellotti" you have no other choice than to make them at home. This traditional recipe is excellent.

At one time it was a tradition to make the sauce with a little of the stuffing cooked with tomato sauce: I do recommend this option.

Crespelle alla fiorentina
Florentine crepes

Ingredients for 4 people

For the crepes:
- Flour: 100g/ 3½ oz/ ¾ cup
- 2 eggs
- Milk: 1 cup
- Butter: 50 g/ 1¾ oz/ ¼ cup
- Salt

For the filling:
- Spinach: 300 g/ 11 oz
- Ricotta: 200 g/ 7 oz
- 2 tablespoons grated Parmesan
- 1 egg
- Nutmeg
- Salt and pepper

For the béchamel sauce:
- Flour: 50 g/ 1¾ oz/ ½ cup
- Butter: 50 g/ 1¾ oz/ ¼ cup
- Milk: ½ litre/ 1 pint/ 2 cups
- 4 tablespoons tomato sauce
- Salt and pepper

- Boil the spinach, squeeze the water out and chop finely, then place in a bowl; add all the other ingredients and mix well.
- Prepare the batter by mixing together the flour, the eggs and salt, then add the milk and melted butter, a little at a time. Mix well and leave to stand for half an hour.
- Fry 8 small omelettes in a little butter in a nonstick frying pan.
- Fill with the mixture and roll up.
- Grease the bottom of a flameproof pan with a little butter and place the crepes in this. Cover with the béchamel sauce, prepared with the ingredients listed above (for the recipe, see the chapter on sauces) and put small spoonfuls of tomato sauce over the top.
- Place in a moderate oven (175°C/ 350°F/ gas 4) for about 20 minutes.

The name "crespella" is of antique origin and derives from "crespo, raggrinzito", meaning wrinkled, creased.

*In the countryside around Florence, this dish was called "**Pezzole della nonna**" (granny's handkerchiefs). Today it is served in all restaurants in Florence.*

Maccheroni ai funghi
Fresh egg noodles with mushrooms

Ingredients for 4 people

- Wide egg noodles, like "pappardelle": 400 g/ 14 oz
- Fresh wild "porcini" mushrooms: 200 g/ 7 oz
- 2 garlic cloves
- Ripe or canned tomatoes: 200 g/ 7 oz/ 1 cup
- ½ glass white wine
- Parsley
- Olive oil
- Salt and pepper

- Sauté the crushed garlic cloves in 4 tablespoons of oil; as soon as they begin to colour, add the white wine and reduce, then add the roughly chopped tomatoes. Salt and pepper.
- After a quarter of an hour, remove the garlic and add the mushrooms, having previously washed and chopped them finely, together with some finely chopped parsley. Cook slowly.
- Boil the maccheroni "al dente", drain and add to the pan with the sauce: stir briefly over the heat and serve boiling hot, sprinkled, if desired, with a little grated Parmesan.

If fresh porcini are not available, you can use dried porcini mushrooms (60 g/ 2 oz) previously soaked in one cup of warm water. Always filter this water before using with the chopped mushrooms.

Maccheroni alla Medici
Medici maccheroni

Ingredients for 4 people

- Wide egg noodles, like "pappardelle": 400 g/ 14 oz
- Butter: 100 g/ 3½ oz/½ cup
- Half a chicken breast
- 4 tablespoons boiled or canned peas
- White truffle (if available)
- Grated Parmesan
- Salt and pepper

- Boil the chicken breast, leave to cool and cut into small cubes; then sauté in a pan with a little butter.
- Add a little hot water and the boiled peas, salt, pepper and then cook for about 10 minutes.
- Cook the noodles until "al dente", drain and place directly into the sauce, stir briefly then transfer into a heated serving platter.
- Top with thin slices of white truffle and serve boiling hot.

Pappardelle con l'anatra
Wide noodles with duck sauce

Ingredients for 4 people

- Wide egg noodles "pappardelle": 400 g/ 14 oz
- Half a duckling (with liver and heart)
- Pancetta or bacon: 50 g/ 1¾ oz
- Ripe or canned tomatoes: 450 g/ 1 lb
- 1 onion
- 1 carrot
- 1 stalk celery
- Parsley
- 1 glass white wine
- Grated Parmesan
- Olive oil
- Salt and pepper

- Sauté the finely chopped carrot, onion, celery and bacon in 4 tablespoons of oil and before these begin to colour, add the duckling cut into quarters, the heart and the liver.

- Cook for a little, add the white wine and reduce completely.
- At this point add the tomatoes; salt, pepper and cook slowly for about one hour.

Remove the pieces of duckling, skin and bone completely, then chop up the flesh, the heart and the liver and replace in the sauce. After a few minutes this will be ready.

- Cook the pappardelle "al dente", drain and add to the sauce, serve sprinkled with grated cheese.

This recipe comes from the countryside around Florence, it can be prepared also with gosling and pheasant.

This dish, rich and filling, was prepared at the end of June and beginning of July, to celebrate the threshing of the wheat.

Maccheroni and pappardelle

Pasta is not usually found in Florentine traditional cooking. Excluding "penne strascicate" and "ravioli", one does not find any other typical pasta dishes.

Home made pasta is not often prepared and it usually contains less eggs than the other classic Italian recipes.

This fresh pasta, however, is used for two excellent dishes of antique origin: maccheroni and pappardelle.

Over the centuries "gnocchi", "spaghetti", "penne", "rigatoni", etc. have all been called "maccheroni". In Florence, maccheroni are wide ribbons, like "tagliatelle" but about 3 cm/ 1¼ inches wide.

"Pappardelle", on the other hand, are wider: about 4 to 5 cm/ 2 inches.

The pasta dough is always the same: for 4 people, you need 400 g/ 14 oz/ 3 cups of flour, 3 eggs, a little cold water, a couple of tablespoons of oil and a pinch of salt.

Maccheroni is served with game sauce, which is always made with carrot, onion and celery, giblets, broth and little tomato sauce.

The pasta, once boiled, should be drained, put into the sauce and stirred over the heat.

Another typical dish is "**maccheroni with rabbit sauce**", made with the sauce of rabbit stew, cooked together with its lungs and livers.

Pappardelle sulla lepre

Wide noodles with hare sauce

Ingredients for 4 people

- Fresh "pappardelle" (see note above): 400 g/ 14 oz
- ½ young hare (with heart, liver, lungs and blood)
- Pancetta or bacon: 50 g/ 1¾ oz
- 1 carrot
- 1 onion
- 1 stalk celery
- 1 sprig parsley
- 1 glass red wine
- Grated Parmesan
- Olive oil
- Salt and pepper

- Chop the celery, onion, carrot and bacon finely and sauté in 4 tablespoons of oil; when these begin to colour, add the roughly chopped hare and the finely chopped heart and lungs.
- Cook for a little to reduce, then add the wine; dilute the blood in a little hot water and add to the pan.
- Continue until the pieces of hare are cooked, then remove from the pan and bone carefully; replace the chopped flesh and finely sliced liver into the sauce.
- Salt, pepper and cook for a few more minutes.
- Boil the pappardelle "al dente" and serve with the piping hot hare sauce.

These should be served with lots of grated Parmesan and, an extreme luxury, topped with very thin slices of truffle.

Perhaps you will be surprised not to find any tomato sauce in this recipe, particularly since you always find tomato in the pappardelle prepared in restaurants.

As a matter of fact, in traditional hare sauce, the tomato is substituted with the blood of the hare.

Considering that this dish was apparently very popular with the Etruscans, there can be no doubt that tomatoes had nothing to do with it, since, being of American origin, they did not appear on Florentine tables until 1500.

If hare blood is not available, you can add tomatoes but not too many: 200 g/ 7 oz/ ¾ cup is quite enough.

Penne alla cacciatora
Penne hunter's style

Ingredients for 4 people

- Ridged penne: 350 g/ 12 oz
- Dressed game birds
  (see note below): about
  600 g/ 1¾ lb
- Pancetta or bacon:
  50 g/ 1¾ oz
- ½ onion
- Dried "porcini"
  mushrooms: 25 g/ ¾ oz
- 1 bay leaf
- Sage
- Red wine
- Olive oil
- Salt and pepper

- Cut the game birds into quarters.
- Sauté a finely chopped mixture of onion, bay leaf, sage and bacon in 4 tablespoons of oil and, as soon as the onion begins to soften, add the birds.
- Salt, pepper and add a cup of wine, continue to cook adding water or broth when necessary.
- Bone the birds carefully and finely chop the flesh; put back in the pan and add the mushrooms, previously soaked well and chopped finely.
- Cook for about ten minutes, then add the penne, cooked "al dente" and drained.

For this traditional recipe you can use snipe, woodcock, teal, mallard, grouse or pheasant, according to taste and availability.
I prefer this sauce without tomato, but if you wish, you may add 250 g / 8 oz / 1 cup of canned tomatoes.
Maccheroni and pappardelle are both excellent with this sauce.

Penne alla fiesolana
Penne Fiesole style

Ingredients for 4 people

- Smooth penne: 350 g/ 12 oz
- "Parma" raw ham (sliced): 50 g/ 1¾ oz
- 1 tablespoon flour
- 2 tablespoons butter
- Milk: 1 cup
- Grated Parmesan
- 1 sprig parsley
- Olive oil
- Salt and pepper

- Prepare a quite liquid béchamel sauce with the butter, flour, milk, salt and pepper, then add one spoonful of grated Parmesan.
- Cut the ham into small squares and sauté in 2 tablespoons of oil, add the béchamel and, when these ingredients have been mixed together over the heat, add the penne, cooked "al dente" and drained.
- Salt, pepper and sauté before serving, sprinkle with parsley and more Parmesan.

Fiesole is a very old Etruscan village located on top of the hills north of Florence, however this recipe is quite modern. It is a speciality served in some trattorias; if the Parma ham is not available, you can use cooked ham or bacon.

Penne alle olive nere
Penne with black olives

Ingredients for 4 people

- Smooth penne: 350 g/ 12 oz
- Parma raw ham or pancetta or bacon: 50 g/ 1¾ oz
- Black olives: 150 g/ 5 oz
- Dried "porcini" mushrooms: 25 g/ ¾ oz
- Ripe or canned tomatoes: 300 g/ 1 oz
- 1 garlic clove
- Grated Parmesan
- Olive oil
- Salt and pepper

- In a large pan sauté, in 6 tablespoons of oil, the garlic, the chopped ham, the mushrooms (already soaked and chopped), and the stoned and chopped olives.
- Cook slowly over a low heat for 10 minutes, then add the tomatoes; salt, pepper and then continue to cook slowly for about 20 minutes.
- Cook the penne "al dente", drain and add to the sauce, sauté for a few minutes then serve hot, sprinkled with grated Parmesan.

Penne strascicate
Penne sautéed with meat sauce

Ingredients for 4 people

- Smooth or ridged penne: 350 g/ 12 oz
- Ground (minced) lean beef: 250 g/ 9 oz/ 1 cup
- Canned tomatoes: 400 g/ 14 oz/ 1¾ cup

- 1 onion
- 1 stalk celery
- 1 carrot
- Broth: 1 cup
- Olive oil
- Salt and pepper

- Chop the vegetables finely and then sauté in 5 tablespoons of oil in a large saucepan.
- When these begin to soften, add the ground beef and cook for about half an hour over a low heat adding the broth a little at a time.
- Add the tomatoes and continue to cook slowly for another hour.
- In the meantime, cook the penne and when they are very "al dente" (about half cooked), drain and add to the sauce.
- Leave to flavour over the heat and reduce for about ten minutes, adding a few tablespoons of Parmesan.
- Serve hot with plenty of cheese.

These "penne" are served in all restaurants in Florence.
You can also prepare them with your usual meat sauce or with the one I suggest in the chapter on sauces. It is important that the pasta finishes cooking in the sauce, so that it absorbs all the flavour.

Ravioli
Meatless stuffed pasta

Ingredients for 6 people

For the pasta dough:
- Plain unbleached flour: 450 g/ 1 lb/ 4 cups
- 4 eggs
- Salt

For the stuffing:
- Ricotta: 300 g/ 11 oz
- Spinach: 600 g/ 1¼ lb
- Grated Parmesan: 50 g/ 1¾ oz/ ½ cup
- 2 eggs
- Nutmeg
- Salt and pepper

- Prepare a normal pasta dough with the flour, eggs, a little water and a pinch of salt.
- Whilst the ball of dough, wrapped in plastic wrap, is left to stand for a few minutes in a cool place, prepare the stuffing.
- Boil the spinach in the little water left on the leaves after rinsing.
- Drain well and chop very finely, then add the ricotta, the Parmesan and the eggs; salt, pepper, season with nutmeg and stir well to obtain a smooth, dense mixture.
- Roll out the dough on a floured surface (either with a rolling pin or with the machine) until extremely thin.
- Place teaspoonfuls of the mixture in rows, about 6 cm/ 2½ inches apart; cover with a layer of dough and cut the ravioli with the rim of a glass. Press around the stuffing and seal with a fork.
- Cook in plenty of salted water, drain with a perforated spoon and serve in a large hot bowl with melted butter (this can be flavoured with sage) and Parmesan.
- Before serving, leave to stand for a few minutes. These are delicious topped with fine slices of white truffle.

You can prepare little balls made from the stuffing, then roll them in flour and cook in boiling, salted water.

*Many call these balls ravioli, even though they are not wrapped in the pasta dough, but in Florence, we know them as "**strozzapreti**" or "**strangolapreti**" (priest-throttlers).*

These "naked" ravioli can be served with melted butter and a few leaves of sage, or with meat sauce; always with plenty of Parmesan cheese.

Risotto alla contadina
Farmer's risotto

Ingredients for 4 people

- Rice (Arborio):
  300 g/ 11 oz/ 1¾ cups
- Ripe or canned tomatoes:
  400 g/ 14 oz/ 1¾ cup
- Peas (shelled): 120 g/ 4 oz/
  1 cup
- Broad (Fava) beans
  (shelled): 120 g/ 4 oz/ 1 cup
- 2 courgettes/zucchini
- French (string) beans:
  120 g/ 4 oz
- 1 onion
- 1 carrot
- 1 stalk celery
- 1 bunch parsley
- Parmesan cheese
- Olive oil
- Salt and pepper

- Finely chop the onion, carrot, celery and parsley and then sauté in 4 tablespoons of oil in a casserole.
- When the onion begins to colour, add the tomatoes and the other vegetables (cut the French beans and the courgettes into small pieces)
- Salt, pepper and cook slowly over a low heat for a quarter of an hour, then add the rice.
- Leave to flavour for a little, then bring to the boil, adding every now and then a ladleful of boiling water.
- Serve with grated Parmesan.

This is a delicious risotto which must be made with vegetables in season; those I have mentioned can be substituted with whatever you like, as long as they are very fresh.

Risotto allo spazzacamino
Chimneysweep's risotto

Ingredients for 4 people

- Rice (Arborio): 300 g/ 11 oz/ 1¾ cups
- Boiled red (kidney) beans: 200 g/ 7 oz/ 1 cup
- ¼ Savoy cabbage
- ½ onion
- 1 tablespoon tomato paste
- 1 garlic clove
- Rosemary
- Olive oil
- Salt and pepper

- In a saucepan sauté the finely chopped onion, garlic and rosemary in 4 tablespoons of oil; as soon as these soften add the tomato paste, diluted in a little hot water.
- Add the washed, cleaned and sliced cabbage and after a little, add the rice.
- Salt, pepper and add, every now and then, boiling water; when half cooked, add the beans and continue until the mixture is creamy.
- Serve with more pepper, a little olive oil and, if desired, Parmesan cheese.

Risotto al sugo
Risotto with meat sauce

Ingredients for 4 people

- Rice (Arborio): 300 g/ 11 oz/ 1¼ cups
- Meat sauce (for 4 people)
- Butter: 50 g/ 1¼ oz/ ¼ cup
- Broth: 1 litre/ 1¾ pints/ 4 cups
- ½ onion
- Grated Parmesan

- Place the finely chopped onion in a pot and sauté in the butter; when the onion begins to colour, add the rice and sauté with no water for a little to take flavour, stirring all the time.
- Add the broth, a little at a time. When about half cooked, add more than half the meat sauce and continue to cook as a normal risotto.
- When "al dente", serve hot, covered with the rest of the sauce and plenty of grated Parmesan.

Risotto coi carciofi
Risotto with artichokes

Ingredients for 4 people

- Rice (Arborio): 300 g/ 11 oz/ 1¾ cups
- 4 large artichokes
- 2 garlic cloves
- Butter: 50 g/ 1¾ oz/ ¼ cup
- Grated Parmesan
- Broth: 1 litre/ 1¾ pints/ 4 cups
- Olive oil
- Salt
- Freshly ground black pepper

- Sauté the crushed garlic cloves in half of the butter and 4 tablespoons of oil in a saucepan; before they colour, add the clean, finely sliced artichokes (remove choke and purple leaves and the outer hard leaves carefully), salt and sauté for a few more minutes, adding a little broth.
- Add the rice and "toast" it slightly, then bring to the boil and slowly add the broth; when cooked "al dente", add the rest of the butter and a few tablespoons of Parmesan.
- Serve this creamy dish with pepper and cheese.

Many alter this delicate recipe by adding tomato sauce or canned tomatoes; this is a mistake often found in restaurants. Parsley is the only ingredient to be added, if desired.

Risotto con la trippa
Risotto with tripe

Ingredients for 4 people

- Rice (Arborio): 300 g/ 11 oz/ 1¾ cups
- Tripe: 280 g/ 10 oz
- 2 onions
- 1 carrot
- 1 stalk celery
- Butter: 50 g/ 1¾ oz/ ½ cup
- Grated Parmesan
- Olive oil
- Salt and pepper

- Boil the tripe for about one hour in 1½ litres/ 2½ pints/ 6 cups of salted water with 1 onion, the carrot and the celery; drain and slice finely.
- Remove the vegetables and keep the broth.
- Sauté the other onion in 4 tablespoons of oil and half of the butter; as soon as the onion softens, add the rice and toast for a few minutes.
- Add the tripe and bring to the boil with the broth.
- Finally add the rest of the butter and a few tablespoons of grated Parmesan.

A little tomato paste or 200 g / 7 oz of canned tomatoes can be added to this.

Ravioli

Risotto nero alla fiorentina

Risotto nero alla fiorentina

Florentine "black" risotto with cuttlefish

Ingredients for 4 people

- Rice (Arborio):
  300 g/ 11 oz/ 1¾ cups
- Cuttlefish: 450 g/ 1 lb
- Swiss chard: 450 g/ 1 lb
- ½ onion
- 1 garlic clove

- 1 tablespoon tomato paste
- Broth: 1 litre/ 1¾ pints/
  4 cups
- 1 glass white wine
- Olive oil
- Salt and pepper

- Clean the cuttlefish removing skin, bones, eyes, beak and insides; keep the bag with the black ink.
- Sauté the finely chopped onion and garlic in 4 tablespoons of oil in a saucepan; as soon as these soften add the chopped cuttlefish and the washed and sliced Swiss chard.
- Cook for 5 minutes, add the wine and when this has evaporated, add the rice and the tomato paste diluted in a little hot broth.
- After a few minutes, salt and bring to the boil, adding a little broth at a time. A few minutes before the rice is cooked, add the cuttlefish ink.
- Serve with plenty of pepper and, if desired, grated Parmesan.

You can use frozen cuttlefish or squid; convenient packets of cuttlefish ink are now available in the food stores.

Timballo alla fiorentina
Florentine timbale

Ingredients for 6 people

For the shortcrust pastry:
- Plain white flour: 300 g/ 11 oz/ 2½ cups
- Butter: 150 g/ 5 oz/ ¾ cup
- 1 egg plus 1 egg yolk
- 1 tablespoon sugar
- Salt

For the timbale:
- Smooth or ridged penne: 300 g/ 11 oz
- Grated Parmesan
- 1 egg
- Butter

For the sauce:
- 2 pigeons
- "Parma" raw ham: 50 g/ 1¾ oz
- ½ onion
- Dried "porcini" mushrooms: 25 g/ ¾ oz
- Broth
- Olive oil
- Salt and pepper
- Béchamel sauce: 1 cup

- Firstly, prepare the shortcrust pastry. Knead all the ingredients together without working the dough too much, then prepare a ball and leave to stand for about one hour wrapped in foil in a cool place.
- In the meantime, sauté the finely chopped onion in 6 tablespoons of oil, then add the chopped ham and mushrooms (previously soaked) ; cook for a little, then add the cleaned and quartered pigeons.
- Allow these to take colour, then add the wine. Salt, pepper and add a little broth; then cook for about 40 minutes.
- Bone the pigeons carefully and put the chopped flesh back into the sauce.
- Cook the pasta "al dente", drain and mix with the pigeon sauce.
- Take the shortcrust pastry, divide in two (one part larger than other). With the larger part, line the bottom and sides of a buttered and floured oven pan (about 25 cm. wide).
- Pour the pasta into this, cover with a fairly liquid béchamel sauce.
- Cover the timbale with the other disc of pastry, press the sides together well and brush beaten egg over the top. Before placing in the oven, pierce with a fork to allow any vapour to escape.
- Cook in a moderate oven (175°C/ 350°F gas 4) for about three quarters of an hour and then leave for a few minutes before serving.

Tortelli alla mugellana
Potato stuffed pasta

Ingredients for 6 people

- Plain flour: 450 g/ 1 lb/ 4½ cups
- White potatoes: 600 g/ 1¼ lb
- Bacon: 100 g/ 3½ oz
- 5 eggs
- 2 garlic cloves
- Rosemary
- Nutmeg
- Grated Parmesan
- Olive oil
- Salt and pepper
- Meat or mushroom sauce

- Prepare the dough for the pasta as usual with the flour, 3 eggs, water and salt; make a ball and leave to stand.
- Boil the potatoes, leave to cool, peel and strain through a sieve.
- Sauté the finely chopped bacon, the garlic and a little rosemary in 6 tablespoons of oil in a small saucepan; as soon as the garlic begins to colour, remove together with the rosemary.
- Place the potatoes in a bowl together with the bacon and oil, add 2 eggs, 4 tablespoons of grated Parmesan, a little nutmeg, salt and pepper; stir well and leave to stand.
- Roll out the pasta to form discs about 5 cm/ 2 inches across, place a spoonful of the filling in the middle of each, fold over and seal the border with fork.
- Boil the tortelli in plenty of salted water and serve with a mushroom or meat sauce (they are also excellent with butter and Parmesan); better still try them with a duck or rabbit sauce.

Mugello is a beautiful, mountainous region to the north of Florence close to the Apennines.

Pesci, ranocchi
e chiocciole
Fish, frog's legs
and snails

Anguilla alla Fiorentina
Eel Florentine style

Ingredients for 4 people

- 1 fresh (live) eel
  (on bone with head):
  1,4 Kg/ 3 lb
- 1 glass red wine
- 2 garlic cloves

- 4 sage leaves
- Breadcrumbs
- 1 lemon
- Olive oil
- Salt and pepper

- Slit around the skin of the neck with the tip of a knife, cut the edge loose, then use your left hand to hold the head and with your right (using a rough cloth to avoid slipping) grip the edge of the skin and peel it down over the tail, turning it inside out.
- Slit along the belly and remove the entrails, cut off the head and, having washed it thoroughly, cut into steaks about 6 cm/ 2½ inches long (fishmongers will usually clean and prepare the eel ready for cooking).
- Place the pieces in a single layer on a plate; salt, pepper and trickle with a little oil, then marinate for about one hour.
- Cover the bottom of a baking pan with a thin layer of oil, add the sliced garlic cloves and the sage leaves. Sauté a little over the heat, then add the eel steaks in a single layer, having coated them with the breadcrumbs.
- Sprinkle these with the marinade and place in fairly hot oven (200°C/ 400°F/ gas 6).
- When the steaks have taken colour (this should take about quarter of an hour), turn and add the wine, a little at a time. Discard the garlic as soon as it begins to brown.
- Cook for a further half an hour and, before serving, sprinkle with lemon juice.

Contrary to the general rule, it is better to drink a young red wine with eel; this is the reason for adding red wine to the eel during cooking.

Anguilla arrosto
Roast eel

Ingredients for 4 people

- 1 fresh (live) eel (on bone with head): 1,4 Kg/ 3 lb
- Sage (or bay leaves)
- Breadcrumbs
- 1 onion
- 1 stalk celery
- 1 garlic clove
- Red wine
- Olive oil
- Salt and pepper
- Bread for "crostini"

- Clean and prepare the eel as described in the recipe for Florentine eel, but this time cut the pieces about 5 cm/ 2 inches long.
- Marinate the eel for about two hours in oil, salt, pepper, sprinkled with finely sliced onion, celery and garlic.
- Coat the steaks with breadcrumbs and put on wooden skewers, alternating with slices of baguette-type bread and sage leaves (or bay leaves, if you prefer).
- Grill or bake, basting every now and then with the marinade diluted with a little wine.

If you are using smaller eels, cook them in their skin. They are tastier this way and the steaks can be skinned individually on the plate.

Anguilla con piselli
Eel with peas

Ingredients for 4 people

- Fresh (live) eel: about 1,4 Kg/ 3 lb
- Fresh or canned peas (shelled): 450g/ 1 lb/ 4 cups
- Ripe or canned plum
- tomatoes: 450 g/ 1 lb
- 2 garlic cloves
- Flour
- Olive oil
- Salt and pepper

- Prepare the eel as described in the recipe for Florentine eel.
- Flour the steaks and sauté in 4 tablespoons of oil and the crushed garlic cloves.
- Brown them gently and add the tomatoes, salt and pepper and cook for about quarter of an hour; remove the pieces of eel from the pan and add the shelled peas.
- Cook for about 20 minutes, adding a little water if necessary, then, just before serving, transfer the eel into the pan and reheat.

Some people prepare this eel in exactly the same way as the "anguilla in zimino"; it is also very good like this.

Others prepare it without tomatoes (the peas, in this case, need to be cooked in water or broth), but this is not a Tuscan tradition.

Anguilla in zimino
Eel with Swiss chard

Ingredients for 4 people

- Fresh (live) eel: about 1,4 Kg/ 3 lb
- Swiss chard: about 1 Kg/ 2 lb
- Ripe or canned plum tomatoes: 300 g/ 11 oz
- 1 onion
- 1 stalk celery
- 1 sprig parsley
- 2 garlic cloves
- Olive oil
- Salt and pepper

- Prepare the eel as described in the recipe for Florentine eel and cut into steaks about 5 cm/ 2 inches long.
- Slice the onion and celery finely and sauté together with the whole garlic cloves in 4 tablespoons of oil; when soft, add the eel.
- Sauté on all sides, then add the tomatoes, a little salt and pepper and leave to cook for about a quarter of an hour.
- Remove the eel and place the washed Swiss chard, sliced into thin strips, into the sauce. Cook for 20 minutes (add some water if necessary) and then return the eel to the pan.
- Cook for a further 20 minutes. Serve hot, sprinkled with plenty of freshly ground pepper.

This eel can be served, with the sauce, on toasted slices of bread, rubbed with garlic.

Baccalà alla fiorentina
Salt cod Florentine style

Ingredients for 4 people

- Soaked salt cod: 900 g/2 lb
- Ripe or canned plum tomatoes: 400 g/ 14 oz
- 1 onion
- 3 garlic cloves
- 1 sprig rosemary
- 1 tablespoon finely chopped parsley
- Flour
- Olive oil
- Salt and pepper

- In a pan slowly sauté the finely chopped onion and two whole garlic cloves in 5 tablespoons of oil; when these begin to colour, add the tomatoes. Salt, pepper and leave to cook over a low heat.
- In the meantime, bone, skin, wash and dry the salt cod. Cut into fairly large pieces (about 5 x 7 cm/ 2 x 3 inches), then flour and fry on both sides in very hot oil, to which a garlic clove and a sprig of rosemary have already been added. Drain and place on a piece of kitchen paper to dry.
- When the tomato sauce is ready, place the pieces of fried cod in a single layer, leave to cook for 10 minutes, keeping the heat low. Immediately before serving, sprinkle with the finely chopped parsley.

"Baccalà" is cod, which has been dried in the sun and preserved in salt. Before cooking it needs to be soaked for 24 hours in running water (or in several changes of cold water).

In Italy you can buy "baccalà" already soaked and ready for cooking.

The word "baccalà" comes from the Portuguese "bacalao" which, in turn, derives from the old Flemish word "bakkeljauw" (stick fish).

How to boil salt cod

Take a large, thick piece of good quality salt cod, which has been soaked for a couple of days.

Place in a large pan with a little cold water (this must just cover the cod), half a cup of white wine, a garlic clove, a sprig of parsley and a few peppercorns.

Place over a low heat and bring the water to the boil, simmer for not more than 10 minutes, turn off the heat and leave to stand for 5 minutes.

Drain thoroughly and serve with good olive oil, a little salt if necessary, freshly ground pepper and, if you like, a few drops of lemon juice.

Baccalà coi porri
Salt cod with leeks

Ingredients for 4 people

- Soaked salt cod:
  700 g/ 1½ lb
- Leeks: about 1 Kg/ 2 lb
- Olive oil

- Ripe or canned plum
  tomatoes: 450 g/ 1 lb
- Salt and pepper

- Clean the leeks by removing the roots, the outer leaves but leaving most of the green part (the tender part).
- Slice the leeks quite finely and sauté in a wide pan with 5 tablespoons of oil.
- When these have reduced in size, add the already boned, and skinned cod cut into pieces about 5 cm / 2 inches square.
- Cook for half an hour; salt to taste and, before serving, add plenty of freshly ground pepper.
- This is delicious served with hot "polenta" (cornmeal porridge).

How to prepare the "polenta"

In a large pot, boil 1 litre/ 1¾ pints/ 4 cups of salted water, then add 300 g/ 11 oz/ 2½ cups of cornmeal (maize flour) and mix together.

Simmer for 30 minutes stirring continuously with a wooden spoon until it is thick and smooth.

Turn the polenta out onto a large platter or wooden tray. Serve immediately, still warm.

Baccalà in zimino
Salt cod with Swiss chard

Ingredients for 4 people

- Soaked salt cod:
  700 g/ 1½ lb
- Swiss chard: 700 g/ 1½ lb
- Ripe or canned plum
  tomatoes: 450 g/ 1 lb
- 1 onion

- 1 stalk celery
- 1 carrot
- 2 garlic cloves
- Parsley
- Olive oil
- Salt and pepper

- In a pan, sauté the finely chopped onion, garlic, celery and carrot in 5 tablespoons of oil.
- When the vegetables have softened, add the tomatoes and after a quarter of an hour, add the Swiss chard rinsed and cut into strips.
- Cook slowly for about twenty minutes, then add the scaled, skinned salt cod, cut into pieces 4 cm/ 1½ inches square.
- Salt, pepper and leave to reduce for about ten minutes.

Calamai in zimino
Squid with Swiss chard

Ingredients for 4 people

- Squid: 900g/ 2 lb
- Boiled Swiss chard or
  spinach: 700 g/ 1½ lb
- 1 onion
- 1 carrot
- 1 stalk celery

- 2 garlic cloves
- Parsley
- White wine
- Olive oil
- Salt and pepper

- Finely chop the carrot, celery and onion and sauté in a sauté pan with 6 tablespoons of oil.
- As soon as the vegetables soften, add the squid cut into strips (your fishmonger should sell these ready to cook, otherwise remove the eyes, beak,

bones, entrails and skin).
- Sauté for ten minutes, then add a glass of white wine; allow to evaporate and then add the roughly chopped Swiss chard.
- Salt and pepper generously, cook for about 20 minutes, adding hot water if necessary.
- Wait a few minutes before serving, sprinkling with more pepper.

Surprise! No tomatoes! The ever present vegetable is missing in this recipe. In fact, the authentic and original recipe does not include tomatoes. If you really want to add them, do not exaggerate; I would say that 300 g / 11 oz are quite enough.

The Italian word "calamai" (literally "ink-wells") refers to fish with an ink bag, that is: cuttlefish and squid.

This recipe can be made with any of these.

What is "zimino"?

Salt cod, eel, cuttlefish, squid and other fish can be cooked "in zimino", in other words, stewed with carrot, onion, celery, tomatoes (not always) and Swiss chard or spinach.

The word "zimino" is typically Tuscan and is of uncertain origin. Some believe it comes from the word "cimino" (caraway). Others think that it derives from the Arabic word "samin", which means fat or from the verb "samana", that is "to grease food with melted butter".

This term was already in use in the fourteenth century, but how it reached Florence and why it was used to refer to recipes using fish and vegetables, is an absolute mystery.

Chiocciole in umido
Stewed snails

Ingredients for 4 people

- Garden snails: 48
- Ripe or canned plum tomatoes: 450 g/ 1 lb
- 1 onion
- 1 carrot
- 1 stalk celery
- Chilli pepper
- Mint
- Olive oil
- Salt

- Sauté the finely chopped carrot, onion and celery in 5 tablespoons of oil; add a pinch of chilli and a sprig of mint. When the onion has begun to colour, add the tomatoes. Salt and continue to cook slowly for about 15 minutes.
- Add the snails (already purged and cleaned) and simmer for about 2 hours, adding a little water if necessary.
- Either serve with special snail forks or with wooden toothpicks.

How to prepare wild snails

To purge wild snails is a long and laborious process; so, if you have not bought the snails ready to cook, you should proceed as follows.

Place the snails in a ventilated wooden box with holes and leave to starve for about two days on a bed of flour, cornmeal, oats or salt.

After this, rinse them well in water and vinegar and then place on a table. Wait for the snails to come out of their shells and throw away those which do not move.

Snails, particularly small ones, can be cooked as they are, in their shell. Larger ones should be boiled in water and vinegar before being added to the sauce.

If you wish, you can extract the snails from their shell and remove the black part of the intestine before cooking.

Frittelle di baccalà
Salt cod fritters

Ingredients for 4 people

- Soaked salt cod:
  400 g/ 14 oz
- 1 egg
- Flour: 200 g/ 7 oz/ ¾ cup
- White wine

- Milk
- Olive oil
- Salt and pepper
- Oil for frying

- In a bowl prepare a batter mixing together the flour, the egg, some milk, some wine, 2 tablespoons of oil, a little salt and pepper. This should form a smooth, not too liquid mixture with no lumps. Mix well and leave to stand.
- In the meantime, take the salt cod and scale, bone and skin.
- Chop it finely on a chopping board and transfer into the batter.
- Mix well and leave to stand for a couple of hours. Stir again then drop tablespoons of the mixture into very hot oil in a frying pan.
- Once the fritters are golden on both sides, place on kitchen paper to drain.
- Serve, hot and crispy, with spinach sautéed in garlic and oil.

Pesce finto
False fish

Ingredients for 4 people

- Tuna fish in oil (canned): 250 g/ 9 oz
- Potatoes: 450 g/ 1 lb
- Parsley
- 2 tablespoons capers
- Stoned olives: 100 g/ 3½ oz
- 2 eggs
- Lemon
- Olive oil
- Salt and pepper

- Boil the potatoes in their skins, allow to cool, peel and mash.
- In a bowl, break up the tuna fish and mix with the potato and the chopped parsley. Salt, pepper and stir well.
- Place on a serving platter and mould into the shape of a fish, then clean any excess off the plate with kitchen paper.
- Prepare a mayonnaise of egg yolks, oil, lemon juice, salt and pepper.
- Cover the whole fish carefully with this and garnish with capers and olives.

This was a typical dish for Fridays, when the Church insisted on the "vigilia" (eve); in other words, meat was forbidden. It was tasty, filling and cheap.

Ranocchi alla fiorentina
Frogs' legs Florentine style

Ingredients for 4 people

- Frogs' legs: about 300 g/ 11 lb
- Flour
- 3 eggs
- Salt
- Lemon
- Oil for frying

- If you have not bought ready to cook frogs' legs (fresh or frozen), follow this procedure: cut off the head, skin, trim and remove the breast and the gall bladder, keep only the back legs (and the liver and the delicious eggs).
- Rinse under tap and leave in water for a while.

Anguilla alla fiorentina

Baccalà alla fiorentina

Chiocciole in umido

Seppie ripiene

- Drain and pat dry, then dredge in flour and leave for an hour in a bowl with the beaten eggs and plenty of salt.
- Deep-fry in plenty of boiling oil and when they are crispy, dry on a kitchen paper. Serve hot with lemon slices.

Another way of frying is to repeat the flouring and the dipping in the beaten egg in order to create a sort of thick coat which becomes very crispy when fried. Some add a few tablespoons of cornmeal (fine maize flour) to the plain wheat flour.

Seppie ripiene
Stuffed cuttlefish

Ingredients for 4 people

- 4 cuttlefish: about 250 g/ 9 oz each
- Ricotta: 100 g/ 3½ oz
- Spinach: 200 g/ 7 oz
- 1 egg
- 2 tablespoons Parmesan
- 1 tablespoon flour
- Ripe or canned plum tomatoes: 300 g/ 11 oz
- 1 small onion
- 1 carrot
- 1 stalk celery
- Olive oil
- Salt and pepper

- Clean the cuttlefish by removing the skin, the bone, the eyes, the beak and the entrails; rinse well, taking care to leave the head and the tentacles attached to the sack.
- Boil the spinach, wring dry, chop finely and mix with the ricotta; add the egg, Parmesan, flour, salt and pepper.
- Fill the cuttlefish with this stuffing and sew the sack or close with a toothpick.
- Prepare the sauce by gently frying the finely chopped carrot, onion and celery, then add the tomatoes, salt and pepper.
- Place the cuttlefish in this sauce and cook slowly for about one hour adding a little water, if necessary.

Usually the cuttlefish is not tender. To avoid this, I will now reveal a little fishermen's trick; add one or two corks to the sauce. This might appear strange, yet the flesh of the cuttlefish will melt in your mouth.

The cuttlefish was already served in Florence in the fourteenth century, and there are recipes in the "Libro della cucina del XIV secolo" by an anonymous, yet certainly Florentine, author.

Sogliole alla fiorentina

Sole Florentine style

Ingredients for 4 people

- 2 soles (on bone with head): 400 g/ 14 oz each
- Spinach: 900 g/ 2 lb
- Butter: 100 g/ 3½ oz
- 1 glass white wine
- Flour: 50 g/ 1¾ oz/ ¼ cup
- Milk: ½ litre/ 1 pint/ 2 cups
- Grated Parmesan
- Nutmeg
- Salt and pepper

- Clean the spinach, wash and cook for a few minutes in the water left on the leaves and a little salt; wring out the water well, chop finely and sauté in 30 g/ 1 oz of butter.
- Cut the soles into 8 fillets (this can be done by the fishmonger, or you can use frozen sole fillets) and place in a pan with the wine, 30 g/ 1 oz of butter, salt and pepper.
- Cover and cook very slowly for 10 minutes, then remove and allow the sauce to reduce to 3 tablespoons.
- In the meantime, prepare a béchamel with 30 g/ 1 oz of butter, 30 g/ 1 oz of flour, the milk, salt, pepper and a little nutmeg; add the cooking sauce as well.
- With the remaining butter, grease a flameproof dish, then spread the spinach over the bottom, lay the fillets on this and cover with the béchamel sauce.
- Sprinkle the Parmesan over the top and grill in a hot oven.

Storione ubriaco

Drunken sturgeon

Ingredients for 4 people

- Sturgeon (or dogfish) steaks: 600 g/ 1¼ lb
- 1 lemon
- Parsley
- Rosemary
- 1 glass white wine
- 2 garlic cloves
- Olive oil
- Salt and pepper

- Marinate the steaks for a few hours in oil, salt, pepper, lemon juice, chopped parsley and rosemary.
- Sauté the whole garlic cloves in 4 tablespoons of oil and when these have coloured, add the sturgeon steaks.
- When these have been sautéed on both sides, add the white wine, salt, pepper and leave to reduce.
- When cooked, add a little of the marinade; serve in its own sauce and sprinkle with more chopped parsley.

The sturgeon is a very antique fish. In Italian seas there were once various types which, during the mating season in spring, swam up the rivers (the female sturgeon can produce up to 2 million eggs, commonly known as caviar).

Today they no longer exist in the Arno (the river in Florence), but it seems that two enormous sturgeon (perhaps 200 Kg / 440 lb each), "never seen before by the people" were fished out of the Arno "without difficulty" in 1558, on occasion of Lucrezia de' Medici's wedding with the Prince Alfonso d'Este.

Trota alla chiantigiana
Trout Chianti style

Ingredients for 4 people

- 4 small trout: about 250 g/ 9 oz each
- Butter: 75 g/ 3 oz
- Flour
- White wine
- Lemon
- Parsley
- Salt and white pepper

- Clean the trout by removing the fins and entrails, scrape, wash and dry.
- Stuff these with a mixture of half the butter, a little flour, chopped parsley, salt and pepper.
- Place in a pan and cover with white wine, salt, pepper and cook, uncovered, until the wine has evaporated.
- When cooked, add the rest of the butter, baste with lemon juice and sprinkle with chopped parsley.

Once it was a tradition to add small freshwater crayfish to this recipe. Today these are very rare, but cannot be replaced with prawns or shrimps (seawater fish do not taste good with freshwater fish). Cooking the trout without crayfish causes the dish to lose some of its impressive appearance, but the taste is still excellent.

Trote alla Torrigiani
Trout Torrigiani style

Ingredients for 4 people

- 4 small trout: about 250 g/ 9 oz each
- Gruyere cheese: 200 g/ 7 oz
- 2 egg yolks
- 3 tablespoons milk
- 1 tablespoon chopped parsley
- A sprig thyme
- Breadcrumbs
- Butter: 80 g/ 3 oz
- Salt and pepper

- Clean the trout well: trim the fins, scrape, then take out the entrails, wash and dry.
- Place in a pan and sauté in the butter, parsley and thyme; turn with care and when they are crusty, pour over the beaten egg yolks diluted with the milk and a little salt.
- Cook over a low heat for a few minutes and then sprinkle the trout with grated gruyere, pepper and some breadcrumbs.
- Gratin in the oven.

The recipe for this excellent trout is a personal interpretation of a similar dish invented by the famous Florentine journalist and gourmet Giulio Piccini (better known under his pen-name "Jarro").

This recipe was published, at the beginning of this century, in one of his gastronomic almanacs issued at Christmas.

Carni, pollame e selvaggina
Meat, poultry and game

Agnello al forno
Roast lamb

Ingredients for 6 people

- Baby lamb (leg and saddle): 1,5 Kg/ 3½ lb
- 2 garlic cloves
- 1 large sprig rosemary
- Vinegar
- Olive oil
- Salt and pepper

- Chop the garlic finely, mix together with a tablespoon of salt and of pepper, then add the rosemary leaves.
- Rub the lamb with this mixture, then fold it in two, tying together the saddle and the leg.
- Place in a roasting pan, pour in half a cup of oil and cook in a moderately hot oven (200°C/ 400°F/ gas 6) for at least one hour, basting every now and then with the meat juices from the pan.
- Towards the end, sprinkle with a few tablespoons of vinegar and increase the heat so as to brown the meat on the outside.
- Half an hour before the lamb is done, cut potatoes in large pieces and place them in the pan; they are truly delicious cooked in the lamb sauce.

Lamb has always been a favourite in Florence. In the fourteenth century people loved to eat "spalla di castrone al forno" (roast mutton shoulder), preferring this to the leg; and perhaps they were right.

Roast lamb can also be prepared with "piselli alla fiorentina" (Florentine peas) or with "rapini" (boiled greens such as kale, turnip greens, beet greens), sautéed in the juices of the roast meat.

Agnello alla cacciatora
Lamb hunter's style

Ingredients for 4 people

- Shoulder of baby lamb:
  1 Kg/ 2 lb
- Ripe or canned tomatoes:
  400 g/ 14 oz
- Dry salted black olives:
  100 g/ 3½ oz

- 1 onion
- 2 garlic cloves
- Rosemary
- White wine
- Olive oil
- Salt and pepper

- Bone the shoulder carefully, remove any tendons or tough parts, then cut the meat into pieces.
- Sauté the finely chopped onion, garlic and rosemary in 6 tablespoons of oil in a sauté pan, and when these begin to soften, add the lamb.
- Cook over a high heat and after ten minutes add a cup of wine.
- Allow this to evaporate, then add the tomatoes, salt and pepper. Continue to cook over a low heat for about one hour.
- Towards the end, add the olives.

This dish is usually served on slices of toasted bread.

Agnello in fricassea
Lamb fricassee

Ingredients for 4 people

- Leg or shoulder of baby lamb: 1 Kg/ 2 lb
- 4 egg yolks
- 2 garlic cloves
- Rosemary
- Butter: 50 g/ 1¾ oz/ ¼ cup
- Flour
- A little broth
- White wine
- 1 lemon
- Olive oil
- Salt and pepper

- Sauté the whole garlic cloves and the rosemary in the butter and 4 tablespoons of oil.
- Before the garlic begins to colour, add the lamb boned and chopped into pieces; sprinkle with flour, then brown over a high heat.
- Add a cup of wine and allow to evaporate; salt, pepper and continue to cook, basting every now and then with a little broth.
- Beat the egg yolks with the lemon juice in a bowl; pour this sauce over the lamb when it is cooked.
- Stir well until creamy and after a few minutes, remove from heat. Serve immediately.

At the end, peas, already cooked in water, oil and salt, or sliced porcini mushrooms are usually added.

Anatra all'arancia
Duck with orange sauce

Ingredients for 4 people

- 1 dressed duck of about
  1,2 Kg/ 3 lb (or 2 ducklings)
- 4 oranges
- 1 tablespoon sugar
- 2 garlic cloves
- 1 small onion
- 1 carrot
- 1 stalk celery
- 1 sprig sage
- White wine
- Olive oil
- Salt and pepper

- Stuff the bird with half an orange in sections, a garlic clove, a sprig of sage, salt and pepper; sew together with string securing the wings and legs close to the body.
- Salt and pepper the outside and sprinkle with a little oil. Place in a moderate oven (190°C/ 375°F/ gas 5) and roast for about half an hour, turning and basting with a cup of white wine every so often.
- Remove the duck from the pan and keep hot.
- Add the finely chopped onion, carrot and celery to the meat fat (removing some of the fat if it seems too much), and once the onion begins to colour, add the sugar and the rest of the oranges, skinned and sliced with all the pith removed. Sauté in the fat and then add half a cup of white wine.
- When this has evaporated, strain and heat again, boil for five minutes and then add the duck, divided in quarters. Heat through, adding a little broth if the sauce is too thick (if it is too thin, add a little flour).
- Serve very hot with the creamy sauce and decorated with slices of skinned orange.

Usually, when talking of duck cooked with orange, one immediately thinks of "canard a l'orange", a French dish, famous throughout the world. Once again, we discover that gastronomic theft deprived Tuscan cooking of its claim to fame.

Amongst the Florentine dishes mentioned in the "Libro della cucina del XIV secolo" in the chapter entitled "del Paparo" (about the duck), we can find a description of the "Paparo alla melarancia" (duck in sweet orange sauce). Later, in the Renaissance period, "capon in orange sauce" was one of the Medici's preferred dishes

It was the greedy Catherine de' Medici who taught the cooks of her husband Henry II, the King of France, how to make this Florentine dish.

This recipe is not often found on restaurant menus today, and the combination of the sweet taste of the orange with the gamy taste of the duck is not particularly popular. This is a great shame as it can be, quite delicious, if prepared well.

This recipe can also be used to cook other poultry, such as chicken, guinea-fowl, turkey and pheasant.

Arista alla fiorentina
Roast pork loin Florentine style

Ingredients for 6 people

- Pork sirloin (chump end): 1,5 Kg/ 3½ lb (with bone)
- 2 garlic cloves
- 2 sprigs rosemary
- Olive oil
- Salt and pepper

- Finely chop the rosemary and the garlic and mix with 1 tablespoon of salt and of freshly ground pepper.
- With a very sharp knife, remove the loin from the central bone and spread a little of the mixture on the bone.
- Replace the meat against the bone and tie it tightly with some string. Make a couple of small yet deep holes both into the fillet and the loin, then fill with the flavouring.
- Before placing the pork in the roasting pan, rub more of the mixture on the meat, then sprinkle with oil and place in a moderate oven (175°C/ 350°F/ gas 4).
- Cook for quite a long time, about 2 hours. Baste the meat every now and then with the juices from the bottom of the pan with a spoon.
- Shortly before the meat is completely cooked, increase the temperature of the oven to brown the meat.
- Untie the pork, slice and serve with its sauce.

Half an hour before the pork is ready, I suggest adding 1 Kg/ 2 lb of peeled potatoes cut into large wedges and cooking these in the delicious meat juices.

Arrosto morto
Pan roasted beef

Ingredients for 4 people

- Beef (top rump, rolled back rib): 900g/ 2 lb
- 1 onion
- 1 carrot
- 1 stalk celery

- Bay leaves
- Red wine
- Broth
- Olive oil
- Salt and pepper

- Tie the meat up so that it keeps its form during cooking.
- Sauté the finely chopped onion, carrot and celery in a casserole in 6 tablespoons of oil with a few bay leaves; as soon as the vegetables soften, add the meat and brown over a high heat on all sides.
- Salt, pepper and add a cup of red wine; as soon as this has evaporated, add two ladlefuls of broth and cook slowly for about one and a half hours.
- When the liquid has evaporated, untie the meat, slice and serve with its own hot juices.

The original recipe for "arrosto morto" (dead roast) includes only oil and broth, sometimes there is the addition of garlic and rosemary.

Chicken, rabbit, pigeon and lamb can all be cooked the same way.

The expression "dead roast" refers to the way it was cooked; "live roasts" were those cooked on the spit over the flames.

Bistecca alla fiorentina
Florentine T-bone steak

Ingredients:

- T-bone beef steak:
  900 g/ 2 lb
- Salt
- Freshly ground black
  pepper

- Light a charcoal fire long before you need to cook, so that the charcoals are alive but there is no open flame.
- Place a gridiron which stands about 15 cm/ 6 inches over the charcoals; when heated, place the steak on it. The steak should not be neither washed nor straight from the fridge, but at room temperature.
- Without salt, grill for 6 minutes, then turn over either with a wooden spatula or with tongs, salt and cook for a further 6 minutes.
- Turn once again and salt the other side.
- Place on a wooden chopping board or on a hot plate (avoid cold metal plates) and serve immediately, hot without oil or lemon but with a sprinkling of freshly ground black pepper.

Symbol of Florentine cooking, famed throughout the world, and known outside of Florence as a "fiorentina", our charcoal-cooked steak has teased many expert cooks with its simplicity. Over the years they have tried to give it elaborate but always disappointing recipes.

Let us consider the simple secrets of this Florentine speciality:

***The meat**: preferably Chianine beef aged for 6 days.*

***The cut**: this should be a T-bone with fillet and loin. This cut is difficult to find in Italy outside of Florence.*

***The size**: from 600 to 900g/ 1½ lb to 2 lb and about 2 fingers high. No more, no less; steaks of greater weight are not so successful.*

***The cooking**: very simple. No marinade, and no infusion in oil. Do not wash it, but place it straight on the hot gridiron over live charcoals, with no flame beneath. It should be cooked rare in the centre and well browned on the outside. Remember that steak should not be well done.*

If you wish to eat a good Florentine steak, perhaps it makes sense to eat just that and nothing else. I hate those restaurants in which one orders a steak and they bring only half, apologising that it was too big. Rather a smaller one, but a whole one.

Bistecchine di pecora
Mutton chops

Ingredients for 4 people.

- 4 or 8 young mutton chops
- 2 garlic cloves
- Parsley
- Rosemary
- Vinegar
- Olive oil
- Salt and pepper

- Prepare a sauce made with 4 tablespoons of oil, the crushed garlic, the chopped parsley, a few leaves of rosemary, 4 tablespoons of vinegar, salt and pepper.
- Place the chops in this marinade for a couple of hours, then drain well and place on a hot grate over live charcoals (with no flame), preferably of oak charcoal.
- When well browned, and cooked on both sides, salt and pepper once again.

Typical dish from the area of Campi, a small village West of Florence, where sheep-breeding was an important activity.
For this delicious recipe, you need a young mutton (yearling or winter lamb) about 18 months old.
These mutton chops can also be stewed with tomatoes very slowly.

Braciole con le cipolle
Escalopes with onions

Ingredients for 4 people

- 4 veal escalopes
  of 150 g/ 5 oz each
- 4 medium sized onions
- Olive oil
- Salt and pepper

- In a large pan, sautée the finely sliced onions in 4 tablespoons of oil, when these are golden add the escalopes, washed and still dripping, onto the onions.
- Salt, pepper and cover, then cook over a low heat for one and half hours without stirring.

Braciole di maiale con le olive
Pork chops with olives

Ingredients for 4 people

- 4 pork loin chops of about 200g/ 7 oz each
- Canned plum tomatoes: 400g/ 14 oz
- Black olives: 100g/ 3½ oz
- 1 teaspoon fennel seeds
- 2 garlic cloves
- Olive oil
- Salt and pepper

- In a pan, sauté the chops with the whole garlic cloves and the crushed fennel seeds in 4 tablespoons of oil.
- As soon as they begin to colour, add the tomatoes and the olives. Salt, pepper and cook over a low heat for about 20 minutes.

You can prepare a pork stew in the same way (900 g / 2 lb of pieces from neck or boned cubed leg); in this case, instead of the fennel, it is better to add a large sprig of sage.
The cooking time is about one and a half hours.

Braciole rifatte
Fried escalopes in tomato sauce

Ingredients for 4 people

- 4 veal escalopes of about 150g/ 5 oz each
- Ripe or canned plum tomatoes: 450g/ 1 lb
- 2 eggs
- Breadcrumbs
- 1 garlic clove
- Parsley
- Sage
- A little broth
- Olive oil
- Salt and pepper

- Chop the garlic and parsley finely and sauté in 4 tablespoons of oil, then add the chopped tomatoes. Salt, pepper and leave to cook over a low heat for about 20 minutes.
- In the meantime, beat the slices of meat well (they should become quite large and thin), dip them into the beaten egg, slightly salted, then coat with the breadcrumbs.
- Shake off the excess of breadcrumbs and fry in very hot oil, on both sides, until they are golden.
- Drain, and place in the tomato sauce (this should be a generous quantity); add the sage and cook over a low heat for about half an hour.

Bracioline alla fiorentina
Florentine escalopes

Ingredients for 4 people

- 4 veal escalopes of about 150g/ 5 oz each
- Canned plum tomatoes: 300g/ 11 oz
- ½ onion
- 1 stalk celery
- 1 carrot
- 1 glass red wine
- Olive oil
- Salt and pepper

- Sauté the finely chopped celery, carrot and onion in 4 tablespoons of oil; when the onion begins to turn golden, add the meat and sauté over a high heat, turning often.

Arrosto Morto

Cibreo

- Add the wine, allow this to evaporate completely and add the tomatoes; salt, pepper and cover.
- Continue to cook over a low heat for about 1 hour, adding a little water if necessary.

Cervello alla fiorentina
Brains Florentine style

Ingredients for 4 people

- Calf's brains: 500g/ 1¼ lb
- Butter: 100g/ 3½ oz/ ½ cup
- Flour
- Milk: ½ litre/ 1 pint/ 2½ cups
- 1 egg
- Breadcrumbs
- 1 sprig parsley
- Salt and pepper

- Cook the brains for a few minutes in boiling salted water: peel and leave to soak in cold water for about half an hour then cut into slices about ½ cm/ ¼ inch thick.
- Dip these into beaten egg with a little salt and then coat with the breadcrumbs.
- Place in a frying pan with 80g/ 3 oz of butter and fry until golden.
- Prepare a fairly thin béchamel sauce with milk, 20g/ ½ oz of butter, a tablespoon of flour, milk, salt and pepper.
- Mix in half of the finely chopped parsley, place on a serving dish and pour the boiling hot sauce over the brains.
- Sprinkle with the rest of the parsley.

Cibreo
Giblets fricassee

Ingredients for 4 people

- Chicken giblets (livers, hearts, gizzards, combs, wattles, cock testicles): 400g/ 14 oz
- Butter: 80g/ 3 oz
- 2 egg yolks
- 1 small onion
- Flour
- Lemon
- A little broth
- Chilli pepper
- Salt and pepper

- Finely chop the onion and sauté in butter, as soon as this begins to turn golden, add the giblets, lightly floured (cockcombs and wattles should be boiled and peeled and cut into pieces).
- Salt slightly, pepper, add a pinch of chilli and cook slowly, adding a little broth when necessary.
- After 20 minutes chop everything into pieces and return into the sauté pan.
- Prepare a sauce in a bowl by mixing together the yolks, a little salt, the juice from half a lemon and a little broth.
- Add this sauce to the giblets, mix well, cook for one minute and serve immediately.

This excellent recipe was the pride of Florentine cuisine. Unfortunately it has almost disappeared from our tables.

It is not suited to all tastes, but you should try this old traditional dish. Even its name is interesting.

"Cibreo" (pronounce "cheebrèo) seems to come from the Arabic "zingibereus", which literally means "cooked with ginger fit for a king" or perhaps a more simple translation would be "food fit for a king".

Talking of kings or queens, it is said that Caterina de' Medici, wife to Henry II of France, was an enthusiastic eater of cibreo and she even risked dying from indigestion, having eaten too much.

Nowadays this could not happen since the cockcombs and wattles and, above all, the testicles are extremely difficult to find. The latter are very rare since the chicken are all killed before they grow into cocks.

Coniglio al forno
Roast rabbit

Ingredients for 4 people

- 1 cleaned rabbit of about
  1 Kg/ 2 lb
- Rosemary
- 2 garlic cloves
- White wine
- Olive oil
- Salt and pepper

- Clean the rabbit and put aside the head, the liver, the kidneys and the heart (you can use these to prepare a very good pasta sauce).
- Cut the rabbit into about 12 pieces, wash and dry.
- Place the garlic, rosemary and pieces of rabbit into a baking pan with 6 tablespoons of oil; salt, pepper and roast in the moderate oven (175°C/ 350°F/ gas 4), turning now and then and basting with a little white wine. Cook for 1½ hours.

Roast rabbit can also be cooked whole: maybe it is better looking, but cooked in pieces it is tastier.
In either case I would suggest adding a few potato wedges.

Coniglio alla cacciatora
Rabbit hunter's style

Ingredients for 4 people

- 1 cleaned rabbit of about 1 Kg/ 2½ lb
- Ripe or canned plum tomatoes: 400g/ 14 oz
- Black olives: 200g/ 7 oz
- 2 stalks celery
- 1 onion
- 1 carrot
- 1 sprig parsley
- 1 garlic clove
- ½ cup white wine
- Flour
- Olive oil
- Salt and pepper

- Cut the rabbit into 12 pieces; the hind legs divided into two, the two forelegs and the saddle divided into six.
- Finely chop the carrot, onion, garlic, celery and parsley and sauté in 6 tablespoons of oil.
- When the vegetables begin to soften, add the pieces of rabbit with its chopped liver; sauté for 10 minutes then add the wine.
- When this has evaporated completely, add the tomatoes in pieces and sprinkle with a tablespoon of flour. Salt and pepper to taste, add the olives and cook over a moderate heat or in the oven (190°C/ 375°F/ gas 5) for about one hour, basting with a little broth if necessary.
- This stewed rabbit is excellent served with polenta.

In place of the carrot, onion and celery, you can use a finely chopped mixture of garlic and rosemary. It can also be cooked "in bianco" (literally, "in the white"), without tomatoes, but with broth.

In this case, use only garlic and rosemary and, at the end, add a couple of tablespoons of vinegar.

Coniglio in fricassea
Rabbit fricassee

Ingredients for 4 people

- 1 cleaned rabbit of about 1 Kg/ 2 lb
- Butter: 100g/ 3½ oz/ ½ cup
- ½ onion
- A little broth

- 1 tablespoon flour
- 2 egg yolks
- 1 lemon
- Salt and pepper

- Prepare the rabbit as described in the above recipe and sauté in a casserole, in which you have already sautéed the finely chopped onion in butter.
- Turn continually and when the rabbit is well browned, baste with a little broth; salt, pepper and continue to cook over a low heat for 20 minutes, adding broth when necessary.
- When cooked, thicken the sauce with flour, remove the pan from the heat and, whilst turning, add the eggs beaten with the juice of the lemon; the sauce should be very creamy.
- Serve immediately.

Using this recipe, you can also prepare a veal stew (900 g/ 2 lb of cubed neck or flank or shoulder) to be cooked for one hour.

The term "fricassee" is French, but the original derives from the Latin verb "frigere", meaning "to fry".

Coratella d'agnello
Stewed lambs' sweetbreads

Ingredients for 4 people

- Lambs' sweetbreads, lungs, heart, liver: 700 g/ 1½ lb
- Ripe or canned plum tomatoes: 400 g/ 14 oz
- 2 garlic cloves
- Rosemary
- White wine
- Vinegar
- Olive oil
- Salt and pepper

- Clean every part of the lamb, wash in water and vinegar, then slice finely.
- In a pan, sauté the finely chopped garlic and rosemary in 6 tablespoons of oil; as soon as the garlic begins to colour, add all the sweetbreads; salt, pepper and cook for about 10 minutes.
- Add a cup of white wine and allow to evaporate slowly; then add the tomatoes and cook for a further 40 minutes.

This recipe can also be cooked without tomatoes; in this case, stew with broth. They are also traditionally cooked with artichokes.

*The sweetbreads (and the other parts) can also be floured and fried; this recipe is called "**coratella alla mugellana**".*

Crocchette di filetto
Fillet croquettes

Ingredients for 4 people

- Ground (minced) veal fillet: 400 g/ 14 oz
- Ripe or canned plum tomatoes: 400 g/ 14 oz
- Grated parmesan: 50 g/ 1¾ oz/ ½ cup
- 2 eggs
- A sprig parsley
- Grated lemon rind (only the yellow part)
- Breadcrumbs
- A bunch of basil
- Olive oil
- Salt and pepper
- Nutmeg

- Mix the meat, the eggs, the chopped parsley, the lemon rind and the cheese in a bowl. Salt, pepper and add a pinch of nutmeg.
- Make 12 croquettes with this mixture, roll in the breadcrumbs, shake off the extra and place in a pan with 4 tablespoons of oil.
- Place in a pre-heated hot oven for 5 minutes, turning half way through, then place over the heat.
- When cooked, add the crushed tomatoes and the basil. Salt, pepper and continue to cook for another 20 minutes.

Fagiano alla fiorentina
Florentine pheasant

Ingredients for 4 people

- 1 pheasant
  (male or female) of about
  1 Kg/ 2 lb
- Parma ham:
  150 g/ 5 oz (sliced)

- Bacon: 50 g/ 1¾ oz
- Sage
- White wine
- Olive oil
- Salt and pepper

- Hang the pheasant (having removed the innards) in its feathers for about 3 to 4 days (if it has been hunted, otherwise 2 days in the fridge is enough), then pluck, remove legs and neck, singe and rinse in water and vinegar; dry well.
- Stuff with a mixture of Parma ham (100 g/ 3½ oz), leaving 2 or 3 slices aside for later use, the chopped bacon and sage; salt and pepper.
- Sew up the slit and bard the breast with the rest of the Parma ham and secure with string.
- Place the pheasant in a baking pan, salt, pepper, sprinkle with 4 tablespoons of oil and cook in a hot oven (190°C/ 375°F/ gas 5) for about three quarters of an hour, basting every now and then with white wine.
- As soon as it is cooked, untie, and quarter. Serve hot, together with the ham and the stuffing, and sprinkled with the juices from the pan.

The pheasant can also be covered with unsmoked bacon or pancetta instead of ham, and in this case it known as "fagiano alla pancetta" (pheasant with bacon). You can also stuff with fresh pork sausage.

Fagiano tartufato
Truffled pheasant

Ingredients for 4 people

- 1 pheasant (male or female) of about 1 Kg/ 2 lb
- White truffles
- Fatty raw ham: 50 g/ 1¾ oz
- Finely sliced bacon: 50 g/1 ¾ oz

- Single cream: 200 g/ 7 oz
- Brandy or Cognac
- A little broth
- 2 garlic cloves
- A sprig rosemary
- Sage
- Olive oil
- Salt and pepper

- Prepare the pheasant as described in the recipe above, then stuff with the finely chopped ham, fine slices of truffle and a little salt and pepper.
- Bard the breast with bacon, placing a few leaves of rosemary between the bacon and the skin, secure with string and place in a large pan with garlic, sage and 4 tablespoons of oil.
- Sauté over a high heat on all sides and then add the brandy; continue to cook for about one hour, basting every now and then with a little broth.
- When this is ready, untie, remove the bacon, the rosemary and having quartered it, keep hot on a plate.
- From the sauce in the casserole, remove the garlic and the sage, then add the finely chopped pheasant liver and the cream. Cook for a few minutes and then strain through a sieve.
- Return the pheasant to the casserole and as soon as it is hot, serve on plate, sprinkled with slices of truffle.

This is an antique recipe (it probably originates from the XIV century), of incomparable and exquisite taste!

Faraona al cartoccio
Guinea fowl en papillotes

Ingredients for 4 people

- 1 guinea fowl of about 1 Kg/ 2 lb
- Finely sliced bacon: 100 g/ 3½ oz
- A large piece of pig's caul
- Sage
- 2 garlic cloves
- 4 juniper berries
- Thyme
- Olive oil
- Salt and pepper

- Singe the guinea fowl over a flame, remove the innards, the neck and the claws, then wash thoroughly and dry.
- Stuff with the sage, the crushed juniper berries, the thyme, the garlic cloves, salt and pepper, then cover the breast with the bacon slices, placing a few sage leaves between these and the skin.
- Dip the pig's caul in hot water (to clean and open), spread out on a tea towel in order to dry, then wrap around the guinea fowl, already compactly tied with string.
- Grease some baking paper or foil with a little oil and wrap the bird up completely.
- Place on a baking tray and cook in a moderate oven (175° C/ 350° F/ gas 4).
- After about one and a half hours, remove, and serve still wrapped in the paper.

More simply, the guinea fowl (and also chicken) can be prepared in the following way.
Stuff the bird with a thick piece of bacon and one of cooked ham, cut into little cubes, add a sprig of rosemary, a nut of butter, salt and pepper.
Salt again and wrap in a slightly oiled baking paper. Serve quartered and covered with the stuffing.
*The guinea fowl, once wrapped in the pig's caul, can be cooked in the oven directly without wrapping in the paper; in this case it is known as "**faraona nella rete**" (guinea fowl in pig's caul).*

Fegatelli di maiale
Roast pig's liver

Ingredients for 4 people

- Pig's liver: 450 g/ 1 lb
- Pig's caul (fry): 200 g/ 7 oz
- 1 garlic clove
- Sage
- Bay leaves
- Fennel seeds
- Breadcrumbs
- Crostini- type bread
- Olive oil
- Salt and pepper

- Place the finely chopped garlic, sage, 2 bay leaves in a bowl, add a tablespoon of breadcrumbs, one of crushed fennel seeds, salt and pepper.
- Cut the liver into 12 pieces and roll in this mixture, then wrap, one at a time, in the pig's caul. This should first be soaked in warm water and then spread out on a surface.
- Thread the liver pieces onto wooden skewers about 20 cm/ 8 inches long (it was traditional to remove the leaves and bark from bay twigs and use these) alternating them with crostini and bay leaves.
- Place in a baking tray, sprinkle with oil and cook in a moderate oven (190°C/ 375°F/ gas 5) for about three quarters of an hour, turning occasionally.

If you have secured the caul carefully around the liver, you can also pan roast these in a casserole with a little oil and a little broth (having basted them with red wine).

Fegato alla fiorentina
Calf's liver Florentine style

Ingredients for 4 people

- Calf's liver (sliced finely):
  450 g/ 1 lb
- A sprig of sage
- 2 garlic cloves

- Flour
- Olive oil
- Salt and pepper

- Remove all the nerves and the tough parts from the liver, wash and dry thoroughly.
- Place in a frying pan the whole garlic cloves and the sage with 4 tablespoons of oil; as soon as the garlic begins to colour, add the slightly floured liver slices.
- Cook for a few minutes on each side over a high heat. Only salt and pepper when completely cooked.

In the same way you can prepare tripe, but without the flour and served with grated Parmesan.

Francesina
Left-over boiled beef with onions

Ingredients for 4 people

- Left-over boiled beef: 400 g/ 14 oz
- Onions: 450 g/ 1 lb
- Ripe or canned plum tomatoes: 400 g/ 14 oz
- Sage
- Flour
- Olive oil
- Salt and pepper

- Finely slice the onions and sauté, with the sage leaves, in 4 tablespoons of oil; sprinkle with a tablespoon of flour and as soon as these begin to colour, add the tomatoes.
- Salt, pepper and boil the sauce for about half an hour; add the boiled meat, cut into pieces or slices, then cover the pan and simmer over a low heat for about half an hour, stirring occasionally.
- Serve hot, alone, or with boiled potatoes.

The "lesso rifatto" (re-cooked boiled meat) with onions became known in Florence as "francesina"; there is complete mystery surrounding this name.

I would hazard the following explanation. The dish was obviously of humble origin and maybe its name was to render it more attractive. In the nineteenth century all popular dishes were known as "alla francese" (French style), and the presence of the onions could well have recalled the famous Parisian onion soup.

Fricandò
Fricandeau

Ingredients for 4 people

- Noix (cushion) of veal
  (in one piece): 900 g/ 2 lb
- Parma ham: 50 g/ 1¾ oz
- 1 onion
- 1 carrot
- 1 stalk celery

- Parsley
- 2 cloves
- Butter: 80 g/ 3 oz/ 5 tblsp
- A little broth
- Salt and pepper

- Lard the meat with pieces of ham, then truss up securely so that it keeps its form during cooking.
- In a large pan, place the butter, the onion cut in half, the cloves, the sliced carrot, the celery and the parsley.
- Sauté for a few minutes, then add the meat and brown over a high heat on all sides.
- Cook for about one hour until well done, basting with broth every now and then.
- Remove all the vegetables, slice the meat and serve in its sauce.

This is a simple yet delicious recipe of antique origin, which has unfortunately disappeared from modern Florentine cooking.
The word "fricandò" derives from the French "fricandeau" which in turn comes from the Latin "frigere", in other words, to fry. Today this word usually means a dish of meat cooked in a white sauce.

Fricassea
Fricassee

Ingredients for 4 people

- Veal breast or shoulder: 600 g/ 1¼ lb
- Fresh "porcini" mushrooms: 150 g/ 5 oz (or 30 g/ 1 oz if dried)
- ½ onion
- 1 carrot
- 1 stalk celery
- Parsley
- 2 egg yolks
- ½ lemon
- Butter: 50 g/ 1¾ oz/ ¼ cup
- Flour
- Salt and pepper

- Mix the softened butter with a heaped spoonful of flour, then sauté in a pan together with the carrot, celery and onion tied together in a bunch.
- Add the meat cut into pieces (if you use the breast, leave the bones as well) and, having browned it, add a cup of hot water.
- Salt, pepper and cook slowly for about one hour; then add the sliced mushrooms (already soaked, if using the dried ones) and cook for another half an hour.
- When the meat is tender and well done, remove the bunch of vegetables and pour over a sauce made from the egg yolks beaten with lemon.
- Leave for a minute over the heat, then serve immediately with this creamy sauce.

This authentic recipe for fricassee can be made with chicken, rabbit, lamb or even a mixture of all three.

Germano alla cacciatora
Mallard hunter's style

Ingredients for 4 people

- 1 mallard or teal (wild duck)
- Black olives: 200 g/ 7 oz
- Canned plum tomatoes: 300 g/ 11 oz
- Dried "porcini" mushrooms: 30 g/ 1 oz

- 1 small onion
- 1 carrot
- 1 stalk celery
- A little broth
- Olive oil
- Salt and pepper

- Hang the mallard or wild duck (having removed its innards) in its feathers for 3 to 4 days. Pluck when you are ready to cook, singe over a flame, remove the feet and neck and the glands behind the tail, then rinse in water and vinegar and dry.
- Finely chop the carrot, onion and celery and sauté in 4 spoonfuls of oil; after a quarter of an hour, add the bird, cut into eight pieces.
- Brown and then add the olives and the tomatoes; salt, pepper and cook slowly for about one hour, adding a little broth when necessary.

Involtini al carciofo
Artichoke rolls

Ingredients for 4 people

- 4 veal escalopes of about 120 g/ 4 oz
- 4 thin slices of mortadella sausage
- 1 globe artichoke
- Canned plum tomatoes: 400 g/ 14 oz

- 1 small onion
- 2 medium sized carrots
- 1 stalk celery
- 4 basil leaves
- Olive oil
- Salt and pepper

- Finely chop the onion, carrots and celery and sauté in 5 spoonfuls of oil; as these begin to soften, add the tomatoes and a little salt and pepper.
- While the sauce is cooking, beat the escalopes well (these should increase in size) then place a slice of mortadella on each, add a basil leaf and a quarter of the cleaned artichoke, boiled briefly in salted water.
- Salt, pepper, roll up and secure with two toothpicks.
- Place in the pan with the sauce and cook very slowly for a long time (about 2 hours), adding a little broth when necessary.

Another classic recipe which uses a stuffing of cooked ham and sage is **"Involtini in umido"** *(stewed meat rolls). The rolls (which are smaller, two per person) are sautéed together with the carrot, onion and celery, basted with a little white wine and then cooked with the canned tomatoes.*

Fegatelli di maiale

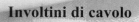

Involtini di cavolo

Involtini di cavolo
Cabbage rolls

Ingredients for 4 people

- 1 Savoy cabbage
- Ground (minced) beef: 300 g/ 11 oz
- Canned tomatoes: 200 g/ 7 oz
- 1 egg
- ½ onion
- 1 garlic clove
- Parsley
- Grated Parmesan
- Nutmeg
- Olive oil
- Salt and pepper

- Mix the ground meat, the egg, a spoonful of Parmesan, the finely chopped parsley, the garlic and a pinch of nutmeg.
- Take the best and largest cabbage leaves, wash and boil briefly in boiling salted water, then drain and spread out on a table.
- Place a spoonful of the stuffing on each one, roll up and secure with string.
- Place these rolls in a fairly deep pan, and sprinkle with the finely chopped onion, 6 spoonfuls of oil, salt and pepper; cover and sauté over a low heat for about twenty minutes.
- When these have turned golden on all sides (take care not to break them), add the strained tomatoes and cook for a further quarter of an hour.
- Remove the string and serve in the pan, sprinkled with grated parmesan.

Lepre in dolceforte
Hare in sweet-sour sauce

Ingredients for 4 people

- ½ hare (or wild rabbit): about 1,5 Kg/ 3 lb
- Pancetta or unsmoked bacon: 50 g/ 1¾ oz
- Grated bitter (unsweetened cooking) chocolate: 30 g/ 1 oz
- Raisins: 40 g/ 1½ oz
- Pine nuts: 30 g/ 1 oz
- Sugar: 20 g/ ¾ oz
- Candied orange or lemon peel: 30 g/ 1 oz
- ½ onion
- 1 carrot
- 2 stalk celery
- Parsley
- Flour
- ½ cup red wine vinegar
- Olive oil
- Salt and pepper

- Finely chop the onion, carrot, celery and pancetta and sauté in 6 spoonfuls of oil, salt and pepper; when these begin to soften, add the hare, cleaned and cut into 12 pieces.
- When this has browned on all sides, drain off a part of the fat, sprinkle the pieces with flour and cook, adding a little hot water or broth every now and then.
- In the meantime, prepare the sweet-sour sauce: put the raisins, the chocolate, the pine nuts, the candied peel, the sugar and the vinegar in a cup.
- Mix well and pour into the pan with the hare. Before serving, allow to boil for 10 minutes.

Sweet and sour sauce tastes better if prepared the day before.
If you wish to simplify this recipe, prepare the sauce with only sugar and vinegar.
The same recipe can be used for wild boar.

Lepre in salmì
Jugged hare

Ingredients for 4 people

- ½ hare: about 1,5 Kg/ 3 lb
- Red wine
- Butter: 50 g/ 1¾ oz/ ¼ cup
- 2 garlic cloves
- 3 bay leaves
- 1 onion
- 1 carrot
- 1 stalk celery
- Thyme
- Olive oil
- Broth
- Salt and pepper

- If you have a whole hare, remove its innards (putting aside the liver, heart and kidneys) and leave to hang, head down, for 3 to 4 days; then skin and remove head and legs.
- Take the hare and divide into eight pieces; having washed these, marinate in half a litre/ 1 pint of wine with a little salt overnight.
- Before cooking, rinse and dry, then place the pieces in a casserole without water; salt, cover and leave over a low heat for about ten minutes. This will cause the flesh to sweat, losing the liquid which tastes strongly of game.
- Pour this liquid away, add the butter, 4 spoonfuls of oil, garlic, thyme, bay leaves, the finely chopped carrot, onion and celery and sauté over a high heat.
- When the pieces are browned on all sides, add a cup of red wine, allow this to evaporate and remove the pieces of hare. Pick out the bay leaves and the thyme and strain the sauce through a sieve.
- Transfer the hare back into the sauce, add the liver, heart and kidneys, having cleaned and chopped them, cook for about one and a half hours over a low heat, adding a little broth when necessary.

Lesso
Boiled meat

Ingredients for 6 people

- Mixed beef: 1.2 Kg/ 2 ½ lb
  (brisket, silverside, flank,
  top rib, skirt)
- 1 calf's foot
- 1 or 2 bones

- 1 onion
- 1 stalk celery
- 2 carrots
- 2 tomatoes
- Salt

- Put all the ingredients, except the foot, in a stockpot with three and a half litres/ 6 pints of water.
- Cover, place over a very low heat and simmer for about one and a half hours; then add the leg and cook for a further hour.
- Before serving, leave to stand in its own broth for half an hour.

Boiled beef can be served with green sauce, "Chianti" mustard or pickles.
The secret of good boiled meat lies in the quality and variety of the cuts of beef used.
The more you use, the tastier it will be; then it must be cooked very, very slowly. Many add half a chicken.

Lingua in dolceforte
Calf's tongue in sweet-sour sauce

Ingredients for 4 people

- 1 calf's tongue of about 900 g/ 2 lb
- Bitter cooking chocolate: 100 g/ 3½ oz
- 2 onions
- 2 carrots
- 2 stalks celery
- 2 tablespoons pine nuts
- Sugar
- Vinegar
- Flour
- Olive oil
- Salt and pepper

- Place the tongue in salted water together with an onion, a carrot and a stalk of celery.
- Simmer very slowly, for about two hours, until the tongue is well cooked; leave to cool in its broth, then skin and cut into slices about 6 mm/ ¼ inch thick.
- In a large pan, sauté the finely chopped carrot, celery and onion in 6 spoonfuls of oil; sprinkle with a spoonful of flour and cook very slowly until soft.
- In the meantime, prepare the sweet and sour sauce in a bowl by mixing together a cup of vinegar, a cup of water, a teaspoon of sugar, the pine nuts and the chocolate grated or in little pieces.
- Pour this into the pan and cook for about ten minutes; then add the slices of tongue and leave over the heat until the sauce turns creamy (about twenty minutes).
- Wait a few minutes (or better still, allow to cool and then re-heat) before serving.

This recipe is delicious but difficult to make. Be particularly exact in measuring out the ingredients (do not change anything) and use very bitter and good quality fitter chocolate. It would be a serious mistake to use cocoa or milk chocolate.

Part of the noble Florentine cuisine, this dish is difficult to find today and is only prepared in a few family kitchens.

Lonze
Stewed offal

Ingredients for 4 people

- Calf's offal (cheek, lips, tail, heart, tongue, etc.): 900 g/ 2 lb
- Ripe or canned plum tomatoes: 400 g/ 14 oz
- 1 onion
- 2 garlic cloves
- Parsley
- 2 cloves
- Cinnamon
- Nutmeg
- Red wine
- Broth
- Olive oil
- Salt and pepper

- Cut the all the meat into strips (skin and joint the tail) and boil for one hour in salted water.
- Sauté a finely chopped mixture of garlic, onion and parsley in 6 spoonfuls of oil.
- As soon as this begins to soften add the well drained pieces of offal and leave to flavour for a few minutes, then pour in a glass of wine and allow to evaporate.
- Add the tomatoes, salt, pepper, garlic, a piece of cinnamon, a pinch of nutmeg and cover.
- Simmer for about 3 hours, adding hot water every now and then.

The Italian term "lonza" usually refers to the finest cuts of pork or beef, but in Florence and in the Mugello, the "lonze" are instead the very poorest parts of the beef stewed in a tomato sauce.

*Similar recipes to the "lonze" can be found in various parts of Tuscany with different names, such as "**cioncia**" and "**grifi**".*

Oca arrosto
Roast goose

Ingredients for 8 people

- A cleaned goose of about 2 Kg/ 5 lb
- Butter: 50 g/ 1¾ oz/ ¼ cup
- Sage
- Rosemary
- Thyme
- White wine
- Olive oil
- Salt and pepper

- Clean the goose (already hung for 4 days in its feathers), singe, wash and dry well; remove neck and feet.
- Prepare a stuffing by mixing together the butter at room temperature with a spoonful of salt, a little pepper and a few finely chopped leaves of rosemary, sage and thyme; put into the bird.
- Tie securely and place on a baking tray, sprinkle with more salt and pepper and a little oil, then add more sage, rosemary and thyme.
- Place in a fairly hot oven (200°C/ 400°F/ gas 6) and, when it has begun to take colour, baste with a cup of wine, then turn down the heat and continue to cook for about 2 hours, pricking every now and then with a fork to allow the fat to run out.
- Before serving, drain off the fat in the baking pan.

Pecora alla campigiana
Stewed mutton

Ingredients for 4 people

- Mutton: 900 g/ 2 lb
- Ripe or canned plum tomatoes: 500 g/ 1¼ lb
- 1 onion
- 1 carrot
- 1 stalk celery
- 1 garlic clove
- Red wine
- Vinegar
- Broth
- Olive oil
- Salt and pepper

- Cut the mutton into fairly large pieces, remove any trace of fat, nerves or tendons, then leave overnight immersed in water and vinegar.
- Drain and place over heat, with a little salt, to sweat.
- Take one piece of meat and chop finely on the chopping board, then place in a pan with 6 spoonfuls of oil and the finely chopped carrot, celery, garlic and onion.
- When this begins to soften, add all the mutton and cook for about ten minutes, then add a cup of wine.
- Salt, pepper and reduce; then add the tomatoes. Cover and cook very slowly for a couple of hours.
- If necessary, add a little hot water; when ready, the meat should be extremely tender.

*"**Sugo di pecora**" (mutton sauce) is served with pasta (maccheroni, pappardelle or penne); this is very tasty and a favourite amongst the older inhabitants of the area around Campi, where there used to be many sheep.*

Peposo alla fornacina
Kiln man's peppery stew

Ingredients for 4 people

- Beef sticking neck (or chuck or rump): 900 g/ 2 lb
- 8 garlic cloves
- Red wine
- 1 spoonful tomato paste
- Salt and pepper

- Cut the meat into pieces as though for a stew (not too small); place in a pan with the whole garlic cloves, a cup of wine, salt, the tomato paste diluted in hot water and 2 heaped tablespoons of very good, freshly ground, black pepper.
- Pour hot water over this until it just covers the meat and place in a moderate oven (170°C/ 320°F/ gas 4); cook, stirring every now and then, for about three hours. If necessary, add extra boiling water.
- When cooked, the peppery stew should be greatly reduced, creamy and tender; if you want, you can serve this on slices of toasted bread.

It is absolutely essential to use the above suggested cuts for this dish, since it is the fat and the nerves which make the beef so tender. In fact, this recipe includes no oil.

The peppery stew originates from Impruneta, a town famous for its earthenware production (jugs and bricks). Here, the kiln men in the evening would place this dish in the kiln, still hot from the day's work, and would find it cooked the next morning.

Pollastro affinocchiato
Chicken with fennel seeds

Ingredients for 4 people

- A chicken of about 1 Kg/ 2 lb
- Bacon: 50 g/ 1¾ oz
- 1 tablespoon fennel seeds
- 2 garlic cloves
- Flour
- 1 cup white wine
- A little broth
- Olive oil
- Salt and pepper

- Clean the chicken well, then divide into 12 pieces.
- Place the whole garlic and the bacon chopped into small cubes into a pan with 4 spoonfuls of oil; when these are sautéed, add the pieces of chicken and brown well over a high heat.
- Salt, pepper and add a spoonful of crushed fennel seeds, sprinkle with a spoonful of flour and when this has been absorbed, pour over a cup of wine.
- Continue to cook for about 40 minutes over a low heat; the sauce should be very creamy, so add a little broth when necessary.

Pollo alla cacciatora
Chicken hunter's style

Ingredients for 4 people

- 1 chicken of about
  1 Kg/ 2lb
- Ripe or canned plum
  tomatoes: 400 g/ 14 oz
- 1 onion
- 2 carrots

- 2 stalks celery
- 1 garlic clove
- 1 cup white wine
- Olive oil
- Salt and pepper

- Clean the chicken and cut into 12 pieces: 2 drumsticks, 2 thighs, and 2 breasts divided into two and the back divided in two.
- Sauté in 4 spoonfuls of oil with the finely chopped carrot, onion, celery and garlic, then add the pieces of chicken and brown over a high heat in an uncovered pan.
- Add the wine and when this has evaporated completely, add the tomatoes; salt, pepper, cover and continue to cook over a low heat for about 40 minutes.

There are many variations of this recipe, the most common being to substitute the carrot, celery and onion with sage, rosemary, garlic and bay leaves. In any case, I would suggest that you add a handful of black olives in brine.
*You can also prepare "**Coniglio alla cacciatora**" (Hunter's rabbit) in the same way.*

Pollo alla diavola
Barbecued chicken

Ingredients for 4 people

- 1 cleaned chicken of
  about 1 Kg/ 2 lb
- Sage

- 1 lemon
- Olive oil
- Salt and pepper

- Cut the chicken in half down the front (of the breast side, do not cut the back side) then open up and press down well with your hands (be careful not to

154

break the bones) so it becomes of uniform thickness.

- Place on a double grid. Make sure it is well spread out and fastened securely between the two sides.
- Oil both sides, then sprinkle with salt, finely chopped sage and plenty of pepper. Grill for about half an hour over the charcoal.
- Turn 4 or 5 times, basting each time with a little oil beaten together with lemon juice to prevent it from drying out.
- Serve immediately, cut into four with slices of lemon.

The saying goes that the name of "Pollo alla diavola" (Devil's chicken) originates from the quantity of pepper used, which caused the eater to send the cook....to the devil!.

It is more likely that this name derives from the method of cooking which takes place right in the middle of the "infernal" flames.

This method of cooking chicken is also called "al mattone" (on the brick) since in place of the double grid, one can use a brick to hold the chicken squashed down over the gridiron.

Pollo con le olive
Chicken with olives

Ingredients for 4 people

- 1 cleaned chicken of about 1 Kg/ 2 lb
- Black olives: 100 g/ 3½ oz
- 1 medium sized onion
- Rosemary
- Garlic
- White wine
- Vinegar
- Olive oil
- Salt and pepper

- Prepare the chicken as described in the recipe for hunter's chicken and sauté together with the finely chopped onion and 4 spoonfuls of oil.
- When the chicken is browned, pour over half a cup of wine and cook slowly for about half an hour in a covered casserole.
- Before removing from the heat, add the olives, some finely chopped rosemary and garlic and 3 tablespoons of good white wine vinegar.
- Cook and reduce for a further five minutes and serve immediately. It's simply delicious!

Pollo fritto
Deep fried chicken

Ingredients for 6 people

- 1 cleaned chicken of about 1 Kg/ 2lb
- Flour
- 2 eggs
- Salt
- Oil for fryng

- Cut the chicken into 14 pieces: 2 drumsticks, 2 thighs in two, 2 wings and the two sides of the breast cut in two and back divided in two.
- Wash the pieces and dry well, then flour and dip in the eggs beaten with a little salt and leave for an hour.
- Place the pieces in a frying pan with plenty of hot, but not boiling oil, and fry over a moderate heat for about quarter of an hour; only raise the heat at the end to brown the skin.
- Salt and dry on kitchen paper.

It is traditional in Florence to serve fried chicken with other fried vegetables, like potatoes, artichokes, tomatoes, courgette (zucchini) and their flowers and boiled cauliflower.
*To make a proper **"fritto misto alla fiorentina"** (Florentine mixed fry) you should add other fried meats to this mouth-watering list, such as brains, sweetbreads and lamb chops (coated with breadcrumbs).*

Polpettine al limone
Meatballs with lemon sauce

Ingredients for 4 people

- Ground (minced) beef loin: 400 g/ 14 oz
- Grated parmesan: 50 g/ 1¾ oz/ 6 tblsp
- Butter: 30 g/ 1 oz/ 2 tblsp
- 1 egg
- 1 garlic clove
- Parsley
- Flour
- 1 lemon
- Olive oil
- Salt and pepper

- In a bowl, mix the meat together with the egg, the cheese, the chopped parsley and a crushed garlic clove, salt and pepper.
- Leave to stand for about one hour and then prepare 12 patties. Flour and place in a sauté pan with the butter and 3 spoonfuls of oil.
- Cook over a very low heat for about half an hour, turning often.
- Pour over the lemon juice and raise the heat, as soon as the sauce begins to boil, remove from heat.
- These are delicious with boiled vegetables.

Polpettone alla fiorentina
Florentine meatloaf

Ingredients for 4 people

- Ground (minced) veal loin: 500 g/ 1 lb
- Parma ham or mortadella: 60 g/ 2 oz
- Butter: 50 g/ 1¾ oz/ ¼ cup
- 1 egg
- ½ onion
- 1 carrot
- 1 stalk celery
- 1 sprig parsley
- Flour
- Olive oil
- Nutmeg
- Salt and pepper

- Mix the ground veal with the finely chopped ham or mortadella and the egg in a mixing bowl.
- Salt, pepper and add a pinch of nutmeg, stir well and, with wet hands, form a loaf. Flour (or coat with breadcrumbs).
- Chop the onion, the carrot, the celery and the parsley finely and sauté with the butter and 3 spoonfuls of oil in a casserole.
- When these have begun to colour, add the meatloaf.
- Sauté on all sides and then add a spoonful of flour dissolved in half a cup of water, cover and simmer over a very low heat, taking care that it does not stick.
- Serve this with its sauce and half a lemon squeezed over the top.

Quaglie alla fiorentina
Florentine quails

Ingredients for 4 people

- 8 quails
- 8 slices of bacon
- Butter: 50 g/ 1¾ oz/ ¼ cup
- A bunch of parsley,
  thyme and bay leaves
- White wine
- A little broth
- 8 slices of bread
- Olive oil
- Salt and pepper

- Clean the quails well, salt and pepper inside, then cover their breasts with slices of bacon; hold the legs to the body and secure these and the bacon with a string.
- Place in a casserole, together with the butter, 3 spoonfuls of oil and the bunch of herbs; sauté over a high heat.
- When these have browned, pour the wine over the top and allow to evaporate. Continue to cook adding a little broth every now and then.
- When the quails are very tender, remove the herbs; untie and serve with their sauce (if there is too much liquid, thicken with a little flour) on toasted bread dipped lightly into the broth on one side only.

Rognoni alla fiorentina
Kidneys Florentine style

Ingredients for 4 people

- Calf kidneys: 500 g/ 1¼ lb
- Butter: 50 g/ 1¾ oz/ ¼ cup
- 1 sprig parsley
- Breadcrumbs
- Olive oil
- Salt and pepper

- Peel off the skin under cold running water, cut into two halves and remove the fat.
- Heat the butter in a pan as soon as this begins to bubble, add the kidneys for a little, then remove from the pan, drain well and dip into a mixture of salt, pepper and chopped parsley.

- Leave for a couple of hours and then coat with the breadcrumbs, sauté in the butter or grill.

Scaloppe alla fiorentina
Veal escalopes Florentine style

Ingredients for 4 people

- 4 veal escalopes of about 100 g/ 3½ oz each
- Spinach: 600 g/ 1¼ lb
- Milk: ½ litre/ 1 pint/ 2 cups
- 4 thin slices of cooked ham
- 4 slices of Fontina cheese
- Flour
- Salt and pepper

- Boil the spinach, squeeze out the water and chop up. Spread out in an ovenproof tray.
- Salt and cover with a layer of béchamel sauce, prepared with the milk, 50 g/ 1¾ oz of flour and 50 g/ 1¾ oz of butter, salt and pepper.
- Flour and sauté the slices of veal.
- Lay these on top of the béchamel and cover each with a slice of cheese and ham. Place in the oven for 10 minutes and serve immediately.

Spezzatino
Stewed beef

Ingredients for 4 people

- Beef or veal (cubed neck or leg): 900 g/ 2 lb
- Ripe or canned plum tomatoes: 450 g/ 1 lb
- 2 garlic cloves
- Rosemary
- 1 cup red wine
- Olive oil
- Salt and pepper

- Cut the meat into cubes about 3,5 cm/ 1½ inches and sauté over a high heat in 4 spoonfuls of oil with garlic and rosemary.
- Stir often and, when the meat is well browned (you will need about a quarter of an hour), pour over the wine, loosen the crust which will have formed on the bottom of the casserole and allow to evaporate completely.
- Add the tomatoes; salt, pepper and bring to the boil, then decrease the heat and cover the casserole. Stir every now and then and add a little water when necessary.
- For the veal, you will need about one hour, but if you are using beef, almost three hours will be necessary (the meat should be very tender).

*This stew, or **"stufato alla fiorentina"** can also be prepared with onion, celery and carrot, but in this case substitute the rosemary with sage leaves.*

It can be served on slices of toasted bread or with potatoes cooked in the sauce, together with the meat.

This recipe was often used by those who could not afford better cuts of meat since the lengthy cooking rendered even the toughest pieces tender.

Having said this, I would recommend the use of the chuck, neck, leg or shoulder; better cuts of meat would make the stew tasteless and tough.

Lepre in dolceforte

Stracotto alla fiorentina

Stracotto alla fiorentina
Florentine pot roast

Ingredients for 6 people

- Beef (rump or rolled topside): 1,2 Kg/ 2½ lb
- Ripe or canned plum tomatoes: 450 g/ 1 lb
- 1 cup red wine
- 1 onion
- 2 stalks celery
- 2 medium sized carrots
- 2 garlic cloves
- Olive oil
- Salt and pepper

- Flavour the meat with salt, pepper and garlic, secure with string, like a salami.
- Place half a cup of oil, the finely chopped onion, carrot and celery in a casserole.
- Add the meat and sauté well on all sides over a high heat.
- Turn continually for about half an hour, add the red wine and, when this has evaporated completely, add the tomatoes.
- Cover the casserole and simmer over a low heat for about two and a half hours, turning the meat often and adding a little water, if necessary.
- When the meat is "stracotto" (very well-cooked), remove from the casserole and keep hot; tip the casserole and remove with a spoon all the fat you can (keep this for making sauces), then strain the rest of the sauce.
- After a few minutes, heat once again, untie the meat and cut into slices; arrange on a serving dish and pour the hot sauce over the top.

Stufato alla sangiovannese
Casseroled veal San Giovanni style

Ingredients for 4 people

- Veal (cubed neck or leg or shoulder): 900 g/ 2 lb
- 1 onion
- Parsley
- Stock made with bones and calf's foot
- Mixed spices (see note below)
- 1 tablespoon tomato paste
- Red wine
- Olive oil
- Salt and pepper

- Place 6 spoonfuls of oil, a finely chopped mixture of onion, parsley, the meat cut into cubes, salt and pepper in a casserole, preferably earthenware.
- Sauté well, stirring often, then add the wine and a spoonful of mixed spices.
- Add the tomato paste diluted in a cup of stock, then continue to cook slowly adding more stock when necessary.
- This stew will need over two hours, the meat should be very tender and the sauce creamy at the end.

The spices necessary for this stew can only be found in San Giovanni Valdarno (this dish is typical of the "Feste del perdono", celebrated during carnival) and no one will reveal the ingredients of this delicious mixture.

Here, however, is my suggestion: crushed cloves, powdered cinnamon, nutmeg, mace and cardamom.

Trippa alla fiorentina
Tripe Florentine style

Ingredients for 4 people

- Dressed calf's tripe: 1 Kg/ 2½ lb
- Ripe or canned plum tomatoes: 300 g/ 11 oz
- 1 onion
- 1 stalk celery
- 1 carrot
- Grated parmesan
- Olive oil
- Salt and pepper

- Sauté the finely chopped onion, carrot and celery in 4 spoonfuls of oil very slowly for about half an hour, then add the tripe, cut into fine strips and cook for about ten minutes.
- Add the tomatoes, salt, pepper, cover and continue to cook for another 40 minutes over a moderate heat.
- Before removing, add two or three spoonfuls of Parmesan and, if necessary, reduce the sauce a little: the tripe should not be liquid.
- Serve very hot, with more Parmesan.

Trippa al sugo
Tripe with meat sauce

Ingredients for 4 people

- Dressed calf's tripe: 900 g/ 2 lb
- Ground (minced) beef: 100 g/ 3½ oz
- Parma raw ham: 50 g/ 1¾ oz
- Canned tomatoes: 450 g/ 1 lb

- 1 onion
- 1 stalk celery
- 1 carrot
- White wine
- Grated Parmesan
- Olive oil
- Salt and pepper

- Finely chop the onion, carrot and celery and sauté over a low heat in 4 spoonfuls of oil; after about a quarter of an hour, add the meat and the chopped ham.
- Cook for a further ten minutes and then add the tripe cut into strips. Leave to flavour for about fifteen minutes, then pour in the wine and, when this has evaporated completely, add the tomatoes and cook for 40 minutes.
- Sprinkle with Parmesan before serving.

*Another recipe for the tripe is called **"Trippa a pollo scappato"** (Tripe in chicken sauce).*

Prepare the "chicken hunter's style", with carrot, onion, celery, tomatoes and broth; when cooked, remove the chicken and add the tripe cut in strips, allow to simmer in the sauce for about 40 minutes and when cooked, add a little butter and plenty of Parmesan.

The chicken should be eaten on one occasion and the tripe on another; the temptation is usually to eat both, one after the other!

Trippa e zampa
Casseroled tripe and calf's foot

Ingredients for 4 people

- Dressed calf's tripe:
  450 g/ 1 lb
- 1 cleaned calf's foot
- 2 onions
- 3 carrots
- 3 stalks celery

- Ripe or canned plum
  tomatoes: 300 g/ 11 oz
- Grated Parmesan
- Olive oil
- Salt and pepper

- Boil the calf's foot (you usually buy this ready to cook) in salted water with an onion, 2 carrots and 2 stalks of celery.
- Cook for about two hours, until the meat begins to come away off the bone; leave to cool then bone and cut the meat into strips.
- Sauté the finely chopped onion, carrot and celery in 6 spoonfuls of oil in a casserole and as soon as these soften, add the sliced tripe and the foot. Leave to flavour for about ten minutes, then add the tomatoes.
- Salt, pepper and cook for a further 40 minutes, pour in a cup of foot stock, uncover and reduce.
- Serve, not too hot, with plenty of grated Parmesan.

You can serve this dish either like tripe or more liquid like a soup; in this case serve on slices of toasted bread.

Zampa alla fiorentina
Calf's foot Florentine style

Ingredients for 6 people

- 4 calf's feet
- Butter: 50 g/ 1¾ oz/ ¼ cup
- 2 egg yolks
- 1 onion
- Grated Parmesan

- 3 ripe or canned plum tomatoes
- Powdered cinnamon
- Olive oil
- Salt and pepper

- Boil the feet (having scraped and cleaned them) in salted water. When these are cooked and the meat begins to come off the bones, leave to cool in their water.
- Bone and cut the meat into strips, then sauté in a pan with the butter, 2 spoonfuls of oil, the finely chopped onion, salt and pepper.
- Leave to flavour, then add the tomatoes, a ladleful of the foot stock and continue to cook slowly until the sauce thickens.
- Just before removing from the heat, add two heaped spoonfuls of Parmesan, the egg yolks and the cinnamon.
- Stir well and serve piping hot with extra Parmesan.

Verdure
e Frittate
Vegetables
and Omelettes

Asparagi alla fiorentina
Florentine asparagus

Ingredients for 4 people

- Asparagus (green):
  1 Kg/ 2 lb
- Butter: 100 g/ 3½ oz/ ½ cup
- 4 eggs

- Grated Parmesan:
  50 g/ 1¾ oz/ ¼ cup
- Salt
- Pepper in a grinder

- Clean the asparagus by scraping the stems well, wash carefully and tie together in a bunch.
- Place upright in a tall pot, then pour in water until it just covers the white part of the stems and add plenty of salt.
- With a perfectly fitting lid, cover and simmer for about 15 minutes without uncovering.
- Remove the asparagus from the heat when still crunchy, drain, untie and remove the tough part of the stems.
- In a fairly large saucepan, melt 50 g/ 2 oz/ ¼ cup of butter and flavour the tips of the asparagus in this for a few minutes; handle them with care, using a wooden spoon.
- Before removing from the heat, sprinkle with Parmesan and freshly ground black pepper.
- Serve the asparagus in their own sauce.
- Fry the eggs in the rest of the butter and lay them over the tips.

Do not completely immerse the asparagus in water because, in this way, much of the flavour is lost and the tips break far more easily (the tips should be steamed).

A few hints about the perfect fried egg: you need to break the egg into the just melted butter, first the white and, when this has begun to coagulate, the yolk in the middle. Salt the white, pepper the yolk and cook over a low heat.

Baccelli alla carnesecca
Broad (fava) beans with bacon

Ingredients for 4 people

- Fresh broad (fava) beans: 2 Kg/ 4 lb (in the pod)
- Bacon or "pancetta": 100 g/ 3½ oz
- 1 small onion
- 1 bunch parsley
- ½ cup white wine
- 1 tablespoon sugar
- A little broth
- Olive oil
- Salt and pepper

- Chop the bacon and onion finely and sauté in a casserole with 5 tablespoons of oil.
- When the onion has turned golden, add the shelled, washed beans; salt, pepper and leave to flavour for about ten minutes.
- Add the wine and when this has evaporated completely, add the sugar and the chopped parsley.
- Leave to cook over a low heat, adding a little broth when necessary.

The bacon (preferably unsmoked) can be replaced with "pancetta" or "Parma" ham.

*With some simple variations (replacing the wine with a cup of broth and adding a little tomato sauce or paste) you can also prepare **"baccelli stufati"** (stewed broad beans).*

"Baccelli" (as fresh broad (fava) beans are called in Florence) are more often eaten raw than cooked, particularly at the beginning of spring when they are not quite ripe, but small, sweet and tender, with "pecorino" (sheep's milk cheese).

Carciofi alla contadina
Artichokes farmer's style

Ingredients for 4 people

- 8 globe artichokes
- Canned plum tomatoes: 300 g/ 11 oz
- 1 garlic clove
- 1 sprig thyme
- Parsley
- Olive oil
- Salt and pepper

- Clean the artichokes by cutting off the stalk (leave 2 cm / 1 in), trimming the spines, and removing the tough outer leaves.
- Cut into 4 or 6 wedges, according to their size, and place in a pan to sauté in 5 tablespoons of oil with the whole garlic clove, the thyme, salt and pepper.
- When they have coloured, remove the garlic, add the tomatoes (or some tomato paste diluted in a ladleful of water), cover and cook over a moderate heat.
- When ready, sprinkle with the chopped parsley.

Carciofi alla fiorentina
Florentine artichokes

Ingredients for 4 people

- 8 large globe artichokes
- Boiled spinach:
  about 200 g/ 7 oz
- Butter: 50 g/ 1¾ oz/ ¼ cup
- 4 tablespoons cream
- Béchamel sauce: 2 cups
- 1 tablespoon flour
- 1 lemon
- Grated Parmesan
- Salt

- Pull off the leaves (you can use these to make an excellent "risotto"), remove the stalk and then the choke to make 8 little "cups" (artichoke bottoms).
- Place immediately in water with lemon juice to prevent discolouration, then boil for 5 minutes in water, to which you have added a little salt and a tablespoon of flour.
- Boil for 10 minutes then transfer to a sauté pan and sauté with the butter, the cream and a little salt.
- Place in a ovenproof dish and fill the bottoms with the spinach. This must be finely chopped and sautéed briefly in the sauce of the artichokes.
- Cover with the béchamel sauce, sprinkle with plenty of grated Parmesan then gratin in the oven.

Carciofi fritti
Deep-fried artichokes

Ingredients for 4 people

- 4 globe artichokes
- 2 eggs
- Flour
- Salt
- 2 lemons
- Oil for frying

- Clean the artichokes by removing the upper part and the outer, tougher leaves but leave 2 cm/ 1 in of stalk.
- Divide each artichoke into two, remove the choke and slice thinly, placing the slices straight into water with lemon juice (to prevent discolouration).
- Drain, dry and flour well; just before frying, dip into the egg beaten with a little salt.
- Place a few at a time into plenty of moderately hot oil and when golden and crispy, transfer to some kitchen paper to dry.
- Serve very hot with a little salt and lemon slices.

Carciofi ritti
"Upright" artichokes

Ingredients for 4 people

- 4 large globe artichokes
- Bacon: 50 g/ 1¾ oz
- 1 garlic clove
- 1 bunch parsley
- 1 lemon (or vinegar)
- Olive oil
- Salt and pepper

- Scrape the artichoke stalks (keep about 5 cm /2 inches), remove the tougher outer leaves and trim the tops and bottoms so that they stand upright.
- Place the artichokes and the pieces of stalk in a saucepan with water and lemon juice (or vinegar) to keep them green.
- In the meantime, finely chop the bacon, garlic, parsley, some artichoke stalks, salt and pepper; fill the artichokes with this mixture, pressing the mixture between the leaves with your fingers.

- Place the artichokes upright in an ovenproof dish (the base downwards); add the stalks and sprinkle with salt and pepper.
- Add half a cup of oil, half a cup of water and place in a moderate oven. Baste every now and then with the sauce.

Cavolo strascicato
Casseroled cauliflower

Ingredients for 4 people

- 1 cauliflower of about 1 Kg/ 2 lb
- Canned plum tomatoes: 300 g/ 11 oz
- Black olives: 100 g/ 3½ oz
- 1 Italian pork sausage
- 1 sprig thyme
- Olive oil
- Vinegar
- Salt and pepper

- Clean the cauliflower and boil for about 15 minutes in hot salted water with a little vinegar (to reduce the nasty smell further, add a piece of stale bread as well).
- Once cooled, divide into little florets (cut the stalk into little pieces) and place in a pan together with 4 tablespoons of oil, the thyme and the skinned sausage, broken into little pieces.
- Sauté for a few minutes, then add the canned tomatoes and the olives; add salt and plenty of pepper and cook for a further 15 minutes; do not cov and stir all the time.

Cipolle al forno
Baked onions

Ingredients for 4 people

- 4 large red or yellow onions
- Parsley
- Olive oil
- Vinegar
- Salt and pepper

- Clean the onions and remove the outer skin, boil in water for about 15 minutes.
- Level top and bottom and then cut in half horizontally.
- With a spoon, remove the heart of the onion, forming little "cups".
- Place in a baking tray, season with chopped parsley, salt and pepper; sprinkle with oil and cook in a moderate oven (170°/ 350°F/ gas 4), basting often with the cooking juices.
- Before serving, sprinkle with a few drops of vinegar.

This is a recipe of antique origin, and makes an excellent accompaniment to boiled meats.

A delicious alternative are **"Cipolle ripiene"** *(stuffed onions). These are served in the same way, but the onion hearts are mixed with a little "mortadella" or cooked ham, boiled Swiss chard and a hard-boiled egg. This should be mixed with 2 tablespoons of breadcrumbs and Parmesan.*

Fagioli al fiasco
Beans in a wine flask

Ingredients for 4 people

- Dried white haricot beans: 350 g/ 12 oz
- 4 leaves of sage
- 2 garlic cloves
- Olive oil
- Salt
- Black peppercorns

- Put the beans into a traditional Chianti wine flask (remove the straw around the flask), then add 4 tablespoons of oil, the sage and the garlic cloves in their skins, a teaspoon of salt and one of peppercorns.
- Add cold water until ¾ of the flask is full, then stop with a well-pressed wad of cotton wool.
- Place the bottle in the ashes of a wood fire, taking care that the beans cook at a constant temperature and never boil; every now and then turn the bottle round so that heat reaches all sides.
- When cooked, the water should have completely evaporated and the oil completely absorbed by the beans.
- Serve with a little salt (if necessary), freshly ground pepper and a dribble of olive oil.

Be careful not to place the "fiasco" directly over the flames as it will explode.

To avoid any disappointment, I warn you that this recipe takes a long cooking time: around 4 hours.

On the other hand, remember that this method of cooking beans was once the norm, when both ovens and heating were from wood burning fires. The "fiasco" was placed in the extinguished, yet still hot, oven in the evening and the next morning, due to the constant heat, the beans were perfectly cooked.

If you do not have a wood fire, you can try to cook these by placing the "fiasco" on a folded tea-towel in a pot with water. The water should just simmer.

One last, but important, piece of advice: use small, round white beans, because the usual haricot beans become to big when cooked and will not pass through the bottle neck.

Fagioli al forno
Baked beans

Ingredients for 4 people

- Dried white haricot
  beans: 450 g/ 1 lb
  (or 1 Kg/ 2 lb fresh
  unshelled)
- Ripe or canned plum
  tomatoes: 300 g/ 11 oz

- Pork rind: 100 g/ 3½ oz
- 1 leek
- 2 garlic cloves
- 1 sprig sage
- Olive oil
- Salt and pepper

- Place the beans in a very large ovenproof tureen with a well-fitting lid; add the scalded pork rind, scraped and sliced, the chopped leek, the garlic cloves in their skins, the peeled tomatoes, 4 tablespoons of oil, the sage, salt and pepper.
- Cover the beans with water by at least 3 fingers; stir well and cover.
- Place in a moderate (170°C/ 350°F/ gas 4) oven and do not touch again; only uncover to taste (after about 2 hours) and to check that there is enough sauce.

How to cook dried beans

Take white or red kidney beans (about 100 g/ 4 oz per person) and place in a pot (use a steel pot with a thick bottom), cover with cold water, equivalent to 5 times the weight of the beans (for example, for 4 people you will need 400 g/ 1 lb of beans and 2 litres/ 3½ pints/ 9 cups of water).

Salt, add a clove of garlic, a sprig of sage and 3 tablespoons of olive oil; place over the lowest heat possible. Never raise the heat, but rather lower it still further during cooking.

This is the secret: the water should only just simmer and the beans should hardly move. Remember you can never cook beans in a hurry.

In the old times beans were cooked in the extinguished oven (after the bread had been made) or on one side of the hot plate of old kitchen ranges.

It is impossible to give exact indications of the cooking time needed; it varies from 1 to 3 hours, depending type. In any case, the best way to avoid mistakes is to taste the beans every now and then.

Fagioli all'uccelletto

Spinaci alla fiorentina

Fagioli all'olio
Boiled beans with olive oil

This method of serving beans is so easy that its recipe would seem superfluous . However a few useful hints are necessary.

First of all, boil the beans as mentioned above, then you will need:

- Tuscan extra virgin olive oil
- Salt
- Pepper in a grinder

- 2 tablespoons of cooking water (broth in which the beans have cooked)

- Drain the beans using a perforated ladle and place in a tureen, lightly salt, add freshly ground pepper and sprinkle with plenty of olive oil.
- Leave to stand for a few minutes before serving warm with a few tablespoons of broth and more pepper.

The use of a few drops of vinegar or lemon is controversial (I must honestly admit that in the very oldest Florentine recipes, lemon juice was included), but personally I do not like it and recommend it be added only to black-eyed beans (cowbeans) and cold bean salad.

Beans served like this are a good accompaniment to many dishes, but they are best served with tuna fish or herrings, topped with thin slices of onion.

Fagioli all'uccelletto
Beans cooked like "small birds"

Ingredients for 4 people

- Dried white "cannellini" beans: 400 g/ 1 lb (1 Kg/ 2½ lb fresh unshelled)
- Ripe or canned plum tomatoes: 300 g/ 11 oz
- 1 sprig sage
- 2 garlic cloves
- Olive oil
- Salt and pepper

- In a pot sauté the garlic cloves (not skinned, according to the tradition) and the sage in 5 tablespoons of oil; immediately afterwards add the crushed tomatoes.
- Cook this sauce for about half an hour, then add the beans, having boiled these in cold salted water with a tablespoon of oil.
- Salt, pepper and cook for about a quarter of an hour. The end result should be thick, not liquid.

The name "small birds" refers to the sage, a herb used in cooking small birds.

Fagiolini in umido
French beans with tomato sauce

Ingredients for 4 people

- French (snap, green, string) beans: 900 g/ 1 lb
- Ripe or canned plum tomatoes: 450 g/ 1 lb
- ½ onion
- 1 carrot
- 2 garlic cloves
- Basil
- Olive oil
- Salt and pepper

- Chop the onion and carrot finely and sauté in a saucepan with 5 tablespoons of oil and the whole garlic cloves.
- As soon as the onion softens, remove the garlic and add the washed and trimmed beans.

- Add the crushed tomatoes and the basil; salt, pepper, cover and leave to cook slowly for about one hour until these are cooked and the liquid absorbed.

Green beans sweat during cooking so there is no need to add any water; they should be cooked with only tomatoes and their own juice.

A serious and diffused mistake is to par-boil these in water before placing them in the pan with the tomatoes.

On the other hand it is quite acceptable to cook all the ingredients together: oil, tomatoes, raw beans and a little water.

Fiori fritti
Deep-fried courgette flowers

Ingredients for 4 people

- 12 fresh courgette (zucchini) flowers
- Flour: 100 g/ 3½ oz/ ¾ cup
- 1 egg
- White wine
- Olive oil
- A pinch nutmeg
- Salt
- White pepper
- Oil for frying

- First of all, prepare the batter. This recipe is also excellent for frying other vegetables, such as courgettes, artichokes and tomatoes.
- Place in a mixing bowl the flour, the salt, the pepper, the nutmeg, 3 tablespoons of olive oil and the egg yolk.
- Mix this with half wine, half water until a fairly liquid batter is obtained.
- Leave for about half an hour and, when you are about to use it, add the beaten egg white.
- Remove the stalks, all the green leaves and the internal pistil (some replace this with a piece of anchovy fillet in oil).
- Dip into the batter, drain off excess and fry in plenty of boiling oil. Serve hot and crunchy.

The flowers should be firm and fresh (cook as soon as you have bought them).

Contrary to common theory, the flowers used are not only those attached to courgettes.

Marrows have two sorts of flowers; female flowers with short stalks, which become courgettes or marrows and male flowers, with long, thin stalks, which never become courgettes.

Frittata con gli zoccoli
Omelette with bacon

Ingredients for 4 people

- 6 eggs
- Bacon: 100 g/ 3½ oz
- Olive oil
- Salt and pepper

- Slice the bacon finely and then cut into 2 cm/ 1 inch squares.
- Sauté in a stainless steel or non-stick frying pan together with a little oil; when the lean part has begun to colour, add the eggs beaten together with pepper and a little salt, making sure the squares of bacon are well distributed.
- Cover and finish cooking over a moderate heat; do not turn the omelette, the surface should remain creamy.

This very simple and traditional recipe is popular in Florence and the surrounding area.

There are two main variations: raw, cured ham instead of bacon and butter instead of oil. Some also suggest flipping the omelette over to colour this on both sides.

You can also fold one half of the omelette onto the other half to form a sort of "roll". This method of cooking omelettes was once very popular.

Frittatine trippate
Omelette strips cooked like tripe

Ingredients for 4 people

- Flour: 100 g/ 3½ oz/ ¾ cup
- 3 eggs
- 1 glass milk
- Butter: 70 g/ 2½ oz/ ¼ cup
- Tomato sauce
- 1 bunch parsley
- Grated Parmesan
- Salt

Mix the flour, egg and salt together in a mixing bowl; add the milk and half of the melted butter a little at a time (you can use a mixer for this). Stir well to check there are no lumps.

Heat a piece of butter in a small frying pan (preferably non-stick) and prepare 4 or 5 little omelettes. Once cooked and cooled, slice with a knife into strips about 1 cm/ ½ inch wide.

Put the tomato sauce into a pan (you can also use canned tomatoes sautéed with garlic, oil and basil) and add the omelette slices.

Leave to flavour for a few minutes, add the chopped parsley and sprinkle with Parmesan, just like real tripe.

Funghi fritti
Deep-fried "porcini" mushrooms

Ingredients for 4 people

- Medium sized "porcini" mushrooms: 400 g/ 1 lb
- Flour
- Salt
- Lemon
- Oil for frying

- Remove the stalks of the mushrooms and clean the cap and the stalk, first by scraping with a knife, then rinsing quickly under the tap.
- Dry immediately, then cut the caps and the stalk into thin slices, dredge with flour and fry in plenty of boiling oil.
- Do not cook the mushrooms for too long because they will taste bitter: 4 or 5 minutes is quite enough!
- Place on kitchen paper to dry; salt and serve hot with lemon wedges.

Before frying, some people like to dip these into a batter but I would not advise this since it affects the delicate taste of the mushroom.
Others mix an equal amount of flour with cornmeal.

Funghi in tegame
Stewed mushrooms

Ingredients for 4 people

- Fresh "porcini" mushrooms: 400 g/ 1 lb
- Ripe or canned plum tomatoes: 300 g/ 11 oz
- 2 garlic cloves
- 1 sprig mint or thyme
- Olive oil
- Salt and pepper

- Clean the earth off the mushrooms with a knife, rinse rapidly in cold water and cut both the stalks and the caps into medium sized pieces.
- In a pan, sauté the garlic and the herb in 5 tablespoons of oil; before the garlic begins to colour, add the mushrooms.
- Salt and pepper, then cook slowly with cover; stir every now and then with a wooden spoon.
- When the liquid has completely evaporated, add the tomatoes and cook for about 30 minutes.

This method can also be used as a basis for other recipes: if you replace the tomatoes with 2 egg yolks and the juice of half a lemon, you will have an excellent mushroom fricassee; if, on the other hand, you add neither tomatoes nor eggs but just a handful of chopped parsley, the result will be so-called **"funghi trifolati"** *(sautéed mushrooms).*

Gobbi trippati
Cardoon cooked like tripe

Ingredients for 4 people

- 1 cardoon of about 1 Kg/ 2 lb
- Butter: 100 g/ 3½/ ½ cup
- Grated Parmesan: 100 g/ 3½ oz/ ¾ cup
- 2 garlic cloves
- A little broth
- Flour
- 2 lemons
- Salt

- Cut the stalk into pieces about 7 cm/ 3 inches long, scrape with a knife and remove the strings. As you do this, throw the pieces straight into water with lemon juice or vinegar to prevent discolouration.
- In a pan, dissolve 2 tablespoons of flour in a little cold water (the cardoon will remain white) and then add 1 litre/ 2 pints of water, a tablespoon of salt and the juice of half a lemon.
- As soon as the water boils, add the cardoon and simmer over a low heat until tender (about one hour); then cool, drain and dry.
- In a large sauté pan, melt the butter and the two garlic cloves cut in half, then add the floured stalks. Sauté slightly then continue cooking by adding a little hot broth.
- After 10 minutes, sprinkle with grated parmesan and serve immediately.

The Florentine name "gobbi" (humpbacks), derives from the stooping form of the cardoon ribs.

The "gobbi", once boiled and sautéed with garlic or onion, can also be cooked in a sauce with canned tomatoes and basil.

They are also very good boiled and then deep-fried (dipped in the batter); those left over can be cooked in tomato sauce.

Patate rifatte
"Twice-cooked" potatoes

Ingredients for 4 people

- Potatoes: 900 g/ 2 lb
- Ripe or canned plum tomatoes: 450 g/ 1 lb
- 2 garlic cloves
- Sage
- Olive oil
- Salt and pepper

- Sauté the garlic and sage in 5 tablespoons of oil in a large pan; before the garlic begins to turn golden, add the peeled potatoes cut into large pieces.
- Allow to flavour for a little over a high heat, then add the tomatoes; salt, pepper and finish cooking, adding a little water every now and then, if necessary.

This was a popular dish in all families; it is delicious with boiled meats which, if left over, can be cooked together with the potatoes.

Patate stufate con pancetta
Stewed potatoes with bacon

Ingredients for 4 people

- Potatoes: 900 g/ 1 lb
- Bacon: 100 g/ 3½ oz
- ½ onion
- Sage
- Parsley
- A little broth
- Olive oil
- Salt and pepper

- Chop the onion finely and sauté in a pan with 4 tablespoons of oil, the sage and the chopped bacon.
- As soon as the onion begins to soften, add the potatoes cut into quite large pieces; then sauté for a few minutes over a high heat.
- Add the broth, salt, pepper and finish cooking by, stirring often with a wooden spoon and adding more broth, when necessary.
- Before serving, sprinkle with a handful of chopped parsley.

Piselli alla fiorentina
Peas Florentine style

Ingredients for 4 people

- Fresh green peas (with shell): 1,2 Kg/ 2½ lb (or 450 g/ 1 lb if shelled)
- Bacon: 50 g/ 1¼ oz
- 2 garlic cloves
- 1 bunch parsley
- 1 tablespoon sugar
- Olive oil
- Salt

- Shell the peas and place in a pan with 6 tablespoons of oil, the garlic, the parsley and the salt.
- Add cold water to just cover the peas, leave the pan uncovered and cook over a moderate heat.
- When the peas are almost ready (about 30 minutes), add the sliced bacon and the sugar; leave to cook another 15 minutes and remember that the peas should be served quite liquid.

Piselli al prosciutto
Peas with Parma ham

Ingredients for 4 people

- Fresh green peas: 1,2 Kg/ 2½ lb (or 450 g/ 1 lb if shelled)
- 1 onion
- Parma raw ham: 100 g/ 3½ oz
- A little broth
- 1 bunch parsley
- 1 teaspoon of sugar
- Olive oil
- Salt

- Sauté the chopped onion and the ham cut into small cubes in 6 tablespoons of oil; when the onion turns golden, add the shelled and washed peas.
- Salt, add the chopped parsley, the sugar and continue to cook slowly for around 40 minutes, adding a little hot broth.

Rapini
Sautéed turnip greens

Ingredients for 4 people

- Turnip or beetroot greens (leaves): 900 g/ 2 lb
- 2 garlic cloves
- Olive oil
- Salt and pepper

- Remove the tougher leaves and the ribs of the leaves; wash and place in a pot with salted boiling water (you can also add some turnip cut into pieces).
- Leave uncovered and simmer until the leaves are perfectly cooked (about half an hour).
- Cool by placing the pan under cold running water and then make balls with the leaves by squeezing out the water.
- Sauté the sliced garlic in 6 tablespoons of oil and when this has begun to colour, add the chopped leaves.
- Leave to flavour for about a quarter of an hour over a high heat, turning often and adding salt and pepper.
- Remember that this dish should be rather dry and definitely not watery.

Salviata
Sage and eggs

Ingredients for 4 people

- 6 eggs
- 12 fresh leaves of sage
- Grated Parmesan: 50 g/ 1¾ oz/ 6 tblsp

- 2 tablespoons milk
- 1 tablespoon flour
- 1 tablespoon butter
- Salt

- Beat the eggs in a mixing bowl, then add a tablespoon of flour and mix well. Add the washed and chopped sage leaves, the Parmesan, 2 tablespoons of milk and a pinch of salt.
- Melt a tablespoon of butter in a round ovenproof dish and add the eggs.
- Cook the sage and eggs in the oven, remembering that this is a sort of "egg cake": do not stir, this should be creamy on the surface.

Sedani ripieni
Stuffed celery

Ingredients for 4 people

- 8 large celery stalks
- Ground (minced) veal: 250 g/ 9 oz
- Chicken livers: 150 g/ 5 oz
- Grated Parmesan: 50 g/ 1¾ oz/ ½ cup
- 3 eggs

- Flour
- Butter: 50 g/ 1¾ oz/ 4 tblsp
- 1 small onion
- Olive oil
- Salt and pepper
- Meat sauce

- Clean the stalks by removing leaves, smaller stalks and stringy parts; then boil in boiling salted water. Leave to cool and then cut into pieces about 10 cm/ 4 inches long.
- Sauté the finely chopped onion in the butter, then add the chopped chicken livers and the ground veal; cook for about 15 minutes, stirring all the time.

- Add the egg, the Parmesan, the salt and the pepper and mix into a smooth stuffing.
- Fill each piece of celery and cover with another piece until you have used up all the ingredients. Press and tie together using white string without knots.
- Flour, dip in the beaten eggs with salt and deep-fry in plenty of oil.
- Put a slightly liquid meat sauce in a saucepan, add the fried celery and cook slowly for 20 minutes until the sauce has reduced; untie before serving.

Spinaci alla fiorentina
Spinach Florentine style

Ingredients for 4 people

- Spinach: 900 g/ 2 lb
- Butter: 50 g/ 1¾ oz/ 4 tblsp
- 4 eggs
- 2 garlic cloves
- Béchamel sauce: 2 cups
- Grated Parmesan
- Salt and pepper

- Clean and rinse the spinach well. Do not dry but place directly into a saucepan without water, salt lightly, cover and leave to cook over a moderate heat for about ten minutes.
- When cooked, leave to cool under cold running water and then make balls by squeezing out the water.
- Sauté the two whole garlic cloves in the butter and before these colour, add the spinach; salt and sauté for about ten minutes over a high heat.
- Add about half of the béchamel sauce to the spinach and place in a buttered ovenproof dish; with a spoon make four holes and place one egg in each.
- Salt, pepper and cover with the rest of the béchamel sauce; sprinkle with Parmesan cheese and cook in a hot oven for about 20 minutes.

Tortino di carciofi
Artichoke "egg-cake"

Ingredients for 4 people

- 4 globe artichokes
- 6 eggs
- 1 garlic clove
- 1 bunch parsley

- Flour
- Butter: 50 g/ 1¾ oz/ 4 tblsp
- Salt and pepper

- Clean the artichokes by eliminating the stalks, the spines and leaving the tender leaves.
- Cut the artichokes into thin slices, lightly flour and sauté in a pan with the butter and a garlic clove.
- Salt, pepper and, once the artichokes are cooked, remove the garlic and sprinkle with chopped parsley.
- Place the artichokes slices in an ovenproof dish with their sauce (the dish should be of the right size to make the omelette about 1 cm/ ½ inch thick) and pour the beaten and slightly salted eggs over the top.
- Place in a hot oven and bake until the eggs are firm.
- Serve sprinkled with lemon juice and pepper.

Tortino di patate
Potato cake

Ingredients for 4 people

- Potatoes: 450 g/ 1 lb
- Butter: 100 g/ 3½ oz/ ½ cup
- Grated Parmesan: 50 g/ 1¾ oz/ 6 tblsp
- Flour: 30 g/ 1 oz/ 4 tblsp

- 1 sprig parsley
- 2 eggs
- 2 cups milk
- Breadcrumbs
- Salt and pepper

- Boil the potatoes, allow to cool, peel and cut into slices about ½ cm/ ¼ inch thick; sauté in half of the butter, salt, pepper and place evenly in a buttered ovenproof dish, sprinkled with breadcrumbs.

- Prepare a béchamel sauce with 25 g/ 1 tblsp of butter, the flour and the milk; then add the eggs, salt and the chopped parsley, mix together well and pour over the potatoes.
- Sprinkle with breadcrumbs and garnish with the butter.
- Place in a hot oven until a golden crust has formed.

You can make many other delicious egg cakes by replacing the potatoes with sautéed artichokes or courgettes, or even boiled asparagus or cardoon.

Zucchini al tegame
Sautéed courgettes

Ingredients for 4 people

- Courgettes (zucchini): 900 g/ 2 lb
- Ripe or canned plum tomatoes: 300 g/ 11 oz
- 2 garlic cloves
- Parsley
- Olive oil
- Salt and pepper

- Clean the courgettes, quarter longways and slice into pieces about 5 cm/ 2 inches long.
- Place in pan over a low heat with 6 tablespoons of oil, the garlic and the tomatoes.
- Salt, pepper, cover and cook slowly without adding water. Stir every now and then with a wooden spoon.
- Before removing from heat, add the chopped parsley.

*If you do not wish to add the tomatoes, you will still have a delicious dish, known as **"Zucchini al funghetto"** (courgettes cooked like mushrooms).*

Dolci
Desserts

Biscottini di Prato

Castagnaccio

Africani
African biscuits

Ingredients for 6 people

- 6 egg yolks
- Butter: 50 g/ 1¾ oz/ ¼ cup

- Granulated or castor
  sugar: 180 g/ 6 oz/ ¾ cup

- Beat the yolks well with the sugar and the melted butter (you can use a mixer).
- Take little paper moulds (those used for sweets, biscuits, etc.) about 3 cm/ 1½ inches in diameter and place two tablespoons of the mixture in each.
- Cook in a slow oven (160°C/ 325°F/ gas 2) for about a quarter of an hour; these should turn a deep golden brown, but not really "African black".

The name of this speciality from Chianti and the Mugello derives from the colour of these biscuits when cooked.

They were once considered to be love portents and lovers were advised to eat these before an amorous encounter, together with a glass of Marsala, Vin santo or sweet wine.

Alchermes di Firenze
Florentine Alkermes liqueur

Ingredients for about
2 litres/ 3½ pints

- Pure alcohol (95 GL/ 190 Proof): 600 cc/ 1 pint/ 2 ½ cups
- Sugar: 600 g/ 1¼ lb/ 2½ cups
- Rose water: 150 g/ ¼ pint/ ½ cup
- Cochineal (scale) insect: 2 teaspoons
- Cinnamon: 2 teaspoons
- Coriander seeds: 2 teaspoons
- Mace: 1 teaspoon
- Cardamom: 2 teaspoons
- 4 cloves
- Star anise (flowers): 1 teaspoon
- Vanilla: ½ pod

- Crush all the ingredients (apart from the vanilla which you can cut into pieces) in the mortar and place into a bottle with the alcohol and 300 cc/ ½ pint/ 1¼ cups of pure water.
- Seal the bottle and leave to infuse for a couple of weeks. Remember to shake the bottle once a week.
- After this, dissolve the sugar in ½ litre/ 1 pint/ 2½ cups of cold water and add to the infusion; shake well and leave for another day.
- Filter the liqueur (with a cone of filter paper) and add the rose water.

The ingredients include cochineal, made from the dried body of an insect found only in certain types of oak tree. Its purple colour was used from ancient times to dye materials, whereas today it is only used to colour liqueurs. This antique and traditional Florentine liqueur takes its name from the insect, which is called "alquermes" in Spanish from the Arab "qirmiz" (scarlet).

It seems that this liqueur was a creation of the Medici family, who jealously guarded its secret recipe.

Leone X and Clement VII, both Medici, loved it and called it "Elixir di lunga vita" (Elixir for Long Life) and it was probably imported to France by Marie de' Medici and her alchemist, Ruggieri; in fact, it was known as the "Liqueur de' Medici".

Berlingozzo
Sweet bread

Ingredients for 6 people

- Plain white flour:
  450 g/ 1 lb/ 4 cups
- Granulated sugar:
  200 g/ 7 oz/ ¾ cup
- 2 eggs and 2 yolks
- Butter: 100 g/ 3½ oz/ ½ cup

- Anise liqueur (anisette):
  2 tblsp
- 1 lemon
- Salt
- Baking powder:
  4 teaspoons

- Beat the eggs with the sugar in a mixing bowl (you can use a mixer) and then add the melted butter, the liqueur, a pinch of salt, the baking powder and the grated lemon peel.
- Slowly add the flour until the mixture is like bread dough, knead well and, helped by the flour, make round loaves or long baguettes.
- Place on baking paper and cook in a moderate oven (170°C/ 350°F/ gas 3) for about half an hour, without opening the oven door.

Biscotti di Prato
Biscuits Prato style

**Ingredients for about
40 biscuits**

- Plain white flour:
  450 g/ 1 lb/ 2 cups
- Granulated sugar:
  350 g/ 12 oz/ 1½ cups
- Almonds: 250 g/ 9 oz
  (shelled)

- 3 eggs and 3 yolks
- Butter: 50 g/ 1¾ oz/ ¼ cup
- Baking powder:
  4 teaspoons
- Rum: 2 tablespoons
- Salt

- Place the flour in a heap; at the centre put the sugar, the 3 eggs, the 2 yolks, the rum, the baking powder, the melted butter and a pinch of salt.
- Knead the dough quickly and then add the lightly toasted almonds (not skinned); continue to knead well, flouring your hands every now and then if the dough is sticky.
- Prepare little squashed sticks about 2 fingers wide and 1 cm/ ¼ inch high; place far apart (otherwise they swell up and stick together) on a greased and floured baking tray (or better still, on baking paper) and, having brushed with a beaten egg, place in a moderate oven (180°/ 370°F/ gas 5). A fan ducted oven is perfect for this recipe.
- As soon as they are cooked (about half an hour), cut 1 cm/ ¼ inch apart to obtain the typical Prato biscuit shape.
- Replace in the oven to dry and slightly toast the biscuits.

*These delicious biscuits, also called "**cantucci**", are a speciality from Prato, an important city West of Florence. You can store them for a long time in a tin.*

Bomboloni
Doughnuts

Ingredients for 6 people

- Plain flour: 300 g/ 11 oz/ 2¾ cups
- Butter: 50 g/ 1¾ oz/ ¼ cup
- Yeast (compressed): 30 g/ 1 oz
- Granulated sugar
- 1 lemon
- Salt
- Oil for frying

- Place the flour in a heap on the table and place 50 g/ 1¾ oz/ ¼ cup of sugar, a pinch of salt, grated lemon rind, melted butter and the yeast dissolved in a little warm water in the centre.
- Knead well to obtain a bread-like dough.
- Make a ball and leave to rise in a warm place for two hours in a floured mixing bowl, covered with a tea towel.
- With a rolling pin, roll out the dough on a floured table to obtain a layer about 1 cm/ ½ inch high. Use a cup to cut out circles (knead the left-over pieces together again and cut out more discs).
- Lay a floured tea towel on a flat surface. Place the discs on this, dust with flour and cover with another tea towel, then leave to stand for another hour.
- Fry, a few at a time, in plenty of hot oil (they should float and absolutely not touch the bottom of the pan).
- When they are coloured on one side, turn and when swollen and golden, drain well, dry on absorbent paper towels and roll in castor sugar.

These doughnuts can be eaten like this, or filled with jam or custard cream; they can also be made into rings.

They are similar, but not exactly the same as Krapfen, the latter being made with eggs and milk.

According to popular tradition, the dough for these doughnuts should also include mashed boiled potatoes (equal in weight to the flour) and two eggs, but I think there are very few who follow this recipe.

Castagnaccio
Chestnut cake

Ingredients for 6 people

- Sweet chestnut flour: 450 g/ 1 lb/ 4 cups
- Raisins: 100 g/ 3½ oz
- Pine nuts: 50 g/ 1¾ oz
- Rosemary
- Walnuts: 50 g/ 1¾ oz (shelled)
- 2 tablespoons sugar
- Salt
- Olive oil

- Sieve the chestnut flour into a large mixing bowl, add the sugar and a pinch of salt, then add about ½ litre/ 1 pint/ 2 cups of cold water; stir well to obtain a smooth, quite liquid mixture.
- Add two tablespoons of oil and the soaked raisins; mix well and then pour the mixture into a greased baking tray (this is traditionally rectangular) and large enough to make the chestnut cake about 1,5 cm/ ½ inch thick.
- Sprinkle pine nuts, crushed walnuts and a few leaves of rosemary over the top; before putting into a fairly hot oven (200°C/ 400°F/ gas 6) dribble with about 2 tablespoons of oil.
- Cook for about 30 minutes. The cake is ready when the top is nicely browned, crunchy and the surface rather cracked.

Cenci
Deep-fried sweet "rags"

Ingredients for 6 people

- Flour: 300 g/ 11 oz/ 3 cups
- Sugar: 50 g/ 1 ¾ oz/ ¼ cup
- Butter: 50 g/ 1 ¾ oz/ ¼ cup
- 2 eggs
- 1 lemon (or orange)
- 2 tablespoons sweet wine (Vin santo)
- Salt
- Oil for frying

- Heap the flour and in the centre, place the sugar, the eggs, the grated lemon (or orange) rind, the melted butter (or 4 tablespoons of olive oil) and the Vin santo.

- Knead well for about 10 minutes, then make a ball and leave to stand for about half an hour.
- Using a rolling pin, roll out the dough on a floured surface until about 3 mm/ 1/8 inch thick.
- Cut into strips, two fingers wide, with a knife, then cut again sideways four fingers long so as create diamond shapes.
- Fry in plenty of boiling oil until golden, then dry on kitchen paper.
- Serve hot or cold, sprinkled with sugar (castor or icing).

Cotognata
Quince jam

Ingredients

- Quinces: 3 Kg/ 7 lb
- Granulated sugar: about
  2 Kg/ 5 lb
- Almond oil

- Place the quinces in a ovenproof pan, having washed and dried them, then bake in a hot oven for about half an hour. Peel but do not core, then strain through a sieve.
- Weigh the fruit and place in a pot with the same quantity of sugar; bring to the boil and simmer, stirring constantly. After half an hour the quince jam is ready.
- Grease a rectangular pan with a little almond oil and pour the jam into this. Spread out to form a layer about 2,5 cm/ 1 inch thick.
- Leave to solidify (overnight), then turn out and cut into small squares, rectangles or diamonds, as preferred.
- These pieces of quince jelly should then be rolled in castor sugar. They can be kept in foil.

Dolce Firenze
Bread and butter pudding

Ingredients for 4 people

- Milk: ½ litre/ 1 pint/ 2 cups
- Sugar: 100 g/ 3 ½ oz/ ½ cup
- White bread: 80 g/ 3 oz
- 3 eggs
- Sultanas or raisins: 60 g/ 2 oz
- 1 lemon
- A little butter

- Cut the bread into thin slices, toast slightly then butter whilst hot on both sides and place in the bottom of a flameproof tureen.
- Sprinkle with sultanas, having soaked them in warm water, and the grated lemon rind.
- Beat the eggs well with the sugar in a mixing bowl, then add the milk; pour over the bread and sultanas.
- Cook in a warm oven (150°C/ 300°F/ gas 2) until firm. Serve warm.

Fiorentini
Florentines

Ingredients for 6 people

- Skinned almonds: 300 g/ 11 oz
- Granulated (castor) sugar: 300 g/ 10 oz/ ¾ cup
- Bitter cocoa powder: 150 g/ 5 oz/ 1 cup
- 4 egg whites

- Toast the almonds slightly in the oven and allow to cool.
- Use a food mixer to finely grind the nuts, then mix in the sugar; add the cocoa and mix again.
- Finally add the egg whites and stir well; place tablespoons of the mixture on baking paper (or on a greased and floured baking tray).
- Cook in a low oven for about quarter of an hour.

Frittelle alla fiorentina
Florentine fritters

Ingredients for 6 people

- Plain white flour:
  200 g/ 7 oz/ 2 cups
- Sugar: 50 g/ 1¾ oz/ ½ cup
- Raisins: 80 g/ 3 oz/ ½ cup
- 2 egg yolks
- 1 lemon

- Baking powder: 1 tblsp
- Vin santo (sweet wine):
  1 cup
- Icing sugar
- A little salt
- Oil for frying

- Place the flour and the baking powder in a mixing bowl, then, stirring continually, add the Vin santo and a little water to obtain a fairly thick batter.
- Add a pinch of salt and the two egg yolks, having previously beaten these with the sugar, stir again and add the grated lemon rind and the soaked raisins.
- Place tablespoons of the mixture into plenty of boiling oil.
- When the fritters are golden on both sides, drain well and leave to dry on kitchen paper.
- Before serving, sprinkle with icing sugar.

Frittelle di mele
Apple fritters

Ingredients for 6 people

- Apples (golden delicious): about 500 g/ 1 lb
- Flour: 100 g/ 3½ oz/ 1 cups
- Granulated (castor) sugar: 100 g/ 3½ oz/ ½ cup
- 1 egg
- Baking powder: 1 tblsp
- Vin santo (sweet wine): ½ cup
- Salt
- Olive oil
- Oil for frying

- Prepare the batter by mixing the flour, the egg, 3 tablespoons of olive oil, a pinch of salt and the baking powder diluted in a little warm water.
- Stir the ingredients together, then add the Vin santo (you can replace this with white wine) a little at a time and more warm water until the mixture is quite thin. Leave to stand for at least an hour.
- Peel and core the apples and cut into rings about 3 mm/ 1/8 inch thick.
- Dip into the batter and fry in plenty of boiling oil; when these are golden, leave to dry on kitchen paper and serve sprinkled with plenty of sugar.

These simple apple fritters are delicious. If you wish to give them more flavour, before dipping them into the batter, you can soak the apple rings for about one hour in Vin santo or brandy or rum mixed with some sugar.

Frittelle di riso
Rice fritters

Ingredients for 8 people

- Rice (Italian Arborio): 200 g/ 7 oz/ 1½ cups
- Milk: ½ litre/ 1 pint/ 2 cups
- 2 eggs
- 4 egg yolks
- Flour: 4 tblsp
- Butter: 30 g/ 1 oz/ 2 tblsp
- Raisins: 80 g/ 3 oz/ ½ cup
- Rum or Vin santo: ½ cup
- Baking powder: 1 tblsp
- 1 lemon
- Granulated (castor) sugar
- Salt
- Oil for frying

- Boil the milk with 2 cups of water and a pinch of salt, add the rice and after a few minutes, add the butter, 30 g/ 1 oz/ 3 tblsp of sugar (not more) and the grated lemon rind.
- Simmer until the liquid is completely absorbed, remove from heat and leave the rice to cool.
- Add the egg yolks, baking powder, flour, rum and soaked raisins; mix all the ingredients together well and, just before frying, add the beaten egg whites.
- Take a little of the mixture at a time using a spoon and fry in plenty of boiling oil until golden on both sides.
- Serve these fritters hot, sprinkled with plenty of sugar.

Pandiramerino

Rosemary buns

Ingredients for 6 people

- Plain white flour: 450 g/ 1 lb
- Yeast (compressed): 30 g/ 1 oz
- Sugar: 30 g/ 1 oz/ 2 tblsp
- Raisins: 150 g/ 5 oz
- Rosemary
- Salt
- Olive oil

- Dilute the yeast in a little warm water and pour into the centre of the flour, heaped on a table; add more warm water and knead until the consistency of bread dough.
- Cover with a cloth and leave to rise for about one hour, then knead again well.
- In the meantime, sauté the rosemary and the unsoaked raisins in 4 tablespoons of oil, then remove the rosemary and leave to cool.
- Add the oil, the raisins, the sugar, a few leaves of fresh rosemary and a pinch of salt to the dough and knead again. Divide into little buns, then leave to rise for about half an hour (these should be soft) on a floured baking tray.
- Before baking these buns in a hot oven (200°/ 400°F/ gas 6), make a "cross" with a knife on the top and brush with little oil.

Quaresimali
Lenten biscuits

Ingredients for 6 people

- Sugar: 200 g/ 7 oz/ 1 cup
- Flour: 200 g/ 7 oz/ 1½ cups
- Bitter cocoa powder: 50 g/ 1¾ oz/ ½ cup
- Hazelnut paste: 50 g/ 1¾ oz
- 3 egg whites
- 1 orange
- Powered vanilla or vanillin
- Cinnamon
- Baking powder: 1 tblsp

- Beat the egg whites until firm then add the sugar and the nut paste (this can be replaced with 50 g/ 1¾ oz of hazelnuts, finely ground in the food mixer).
- In a separate bowl, mix the flour with the cocoa, the grated orange rind, a pinch of cinnamon, a little vanilla and the baking powder. Slowly fold this into the egg whites: you should obtain a fairly dense mixture.
- On baking paper (or a buttered tray) form letters of the alphabet with the mixture, using a syringe or confectioner's bag (space well as these will swell with cooking).
- Leave to stand for about one hour, then place in a warm oven (150°C/ 300°F/ gas 2) for about ten minutes.

These nice little biscuits, which you will only find in Italian bakeries during Lent, from Carnival to Easter (once they were the only sweets permitted in this period), are easy to make, even if they are aesthetically less pleasing then those you buy (bakers use special moulds).

Ritortelli d'uova
Orange crepes

Ingredients for 6 people

- 4 eggs
- Butter: 50 g/ 1¾ oz/ ½ cup
- 3 oranges
- 2 tablespoons milk
- 1 tablespoon flour
- Sugar
- Salt

- Beat the eggs with pinch of salt, the flour and the milk; in a buttered non-stick pan make 6 crepes.
- Sprinkle each crepe with a little sugar and with the orange juice and roll up into a cornet.
- Place in a flameproof tray, sprinkle with more sugar, baste with a little orange juice and bake in a hot oven for a few minutes.

This traditional recipe was already used in Florence during the Renaissance period, and we can deduct from this that the very famous French "crepes suzette" are a mere copy of the Florentine original.
To enliven this recipe, you can add orange liqueur or brandy.

Salame dolce
Sweet salami

Ingredients for 6 people

- Dry biscuits: 200 g/ 7 oz
- Sugar: 100 g/ 3 ½ oz/ ½ cup
- Butter: 150 g/ 5 oz/ ¾ cup
- 2 egg yolks
- Bitter cocoa powder: 4 tblsp
- Sweet liqueur (Marsala, Curacao, etc.)

- Beat the sugar together with the egg yolk to obtain a smooth cream; add the melted butter, the cocoa, the liqueur and finally the biscuits, broken up into little pieces.
- Mould this very dense mixture into a salami (or two smaller ones).
- Wrap in foil and leave in the fridge for a couple of hours.
- Serve chilled, cut into slices, like a real salami.

This can be kept for a long time in the fridge, so prepare a large quantity and surprise unexpected guests with this delicious, yet forgotten, delicacy.

Schiacciata alla fiorentina
Florentine flat cake

Ingredients for 6 people

- Plain white flour:
  350 g/ 12 oz/ 3 cups
- Granulated (castor) sugar:
  100 g/ 3½ oz/ ½ cup
- Pork lard: 80 g/ 3 oz
- Yeast (compressed):
  30 g/ 1 oz
- 2 eggs
- 2 egg yolks
- 1 orange
- Powered vanilla or
  vanillin
- Salt
- Icing sugar

- Place the flour in a mixing bowl (or on a table), add the yeast diluted in a little warm water and knead well with your hands. The dough should be quite smooth (add a little water, if necessary).
- Leave to rise in a warm place, covered with a tea towel, for at least one hour.
- In a bowl, add the eggs, the yolks, the lard, the granulated sugar, some vanilla, the grated orange rind and a pinch of salt to the dough.
- Beat vigorously for at least ten minutes with a spoon in a circular movement from top to bottom, allowing as much as air as possible into the batter.
- Pour the mixture into a rectangular baking tray, greased with lard. Choose a tray which will make the flat cake about 2 cm/ 1 inch high.
- Leave again to rise for about 2 hours, covering the tray with a cloth and then bake in a moderate oven (170°C/ 350°F/ gas 5) for about half an hour.
- Once cool, completely cover the "schiacciata" with icing sugar.

This delicious cake can only be found in Florence during Carnival.
It is a very old recipe and once bore the name of "stiacciata unta" (greased flat cake) due to the plentiful use of lard.

Schiacciata con l'uva
Florentine flat cake with grapes

Ingredients for 6 people

- Black grapes (small grape variety): about 1 Kg/ 2 lb
- Plain white flour: 400 g/ 14 oz/ 4 cups
- Yeast (compressed): 30 g/1 oz
- Sugar: 200 g/ 7 oz/ 1 cup
- Olive oil
- Salt

- Slowly dilute the yeast with a little warm water (about half a cup) in a mixing bowl and, stirring all the time, add the flour, 4 tablespoons of oil, 4 tablespoons of sugar and a pinch of salt.
- Knead well and then leave to rise for an hour in a still warm, but switched off, oven.
- Flour a table and roll out the dough with a rolling pin into thin layers (just like home-made pasta), about the shape of the baking tray (traditionally rectangular or square in shape).
- Grease the baking tray with a little oil and line with the dough, leaving the excess dough at the edges; distribute 700 g/ 1½ lb of washed, dried grapes, then sprinkle with two tablespoons of sugar and two of oil.
- Bend the excess dough back over the grapes to cover them (or almost); sprinkle with the remaining grapes, two tablespoons of oil and two of sugar.
- Place in a fairly hot oven (190°C/ 375°F/ gas 5) and bake for about one hour.

This Florentine and Chianti recipe is a traditional "vendemmia" (grape harvest) dish, and is prepared by all bakeries and cake shops in Florence in September and October.

Schiacciata di zibibbo
Flat cake with raisins

Ingredients for 6 people

- Plain white flour:
  400 g/ 14 oz/ 4 cups
- Raisins or sultanas:
  300 g/ 11 oz
- Granulated sugar:
  200 g/ 7 oz/ 1 cup
- Lard: 80 g/ 3 oz

- Yeast (compressed):
  30 g/ 1 oz
- 1 egg
- 1 sprig rosemary
- Olive oil
- Salt

- Place the flour in a mixing bowl and knead together with the yeast diluted in a cupful of warm water and a pinch of salt. Make into a ball, cover with a cloth and leave to rise (the volume should double) in a warm place for about two hours.
- Chop the rosemary leaves roughly and sauté in a little pan together with 8 tablespoons of oil; leave to cool.
- Take the risen dough and knead together with 5 tablespoons of the rosemary oil, the lard, the egg, 100 g/ 3½ oz/ ½ cup of sugar and the soaked and dried raisins; mix well and place the dough in a baking tray.
- Spread out well (it should be about 2 cm/ 1 inch thick), then sprinkle first with the remaining sugar and then with the oil left in the pan, together with other fresh rosemary leaves.
- Bake in a fairly hot oven (190°C/ 375°F/ gas 5) for about 40 minutes. This is delicious hot or cold.

This is the traditional recipe for Florentine flat-cake, yet it is difficult to find today. Similar to "pandiramerino", it is sweeter and more delicious.

For a perfect result, you must use real "zibibbo", in other words large dried sweet grapes with their seeds.

Torta di farina gialla
Cornmeal cake

Ingredients for 6 people

- Plain white flour:
  250 g/ 9 oz/ 2 cups
- Cornmeal (maize flour):
  150 g/ 5 oz/ 1½ cups
- Sugar: 200 g/ 7 oz/ 1 cup
- Butter: 150 g/ 5 oz/ ¾ cup
- 3 egg yolks

- Raisins or sultanas: 100
  g/ 3½ oz
- 1 lemon
- Powered vanilla or
  vanillin
- Salt

- Mix the two flours well and heap on a table, then add the softened butter (leave a little to grease the tray), the sugar, the yolks, the grated lemon rind, the vanilla and the soaked and dried raisins.
- Mix all the ingredients by crumbling in between your fingers for about 10 minutes.
- Place this crumbly mixture in a buttered tray and level out with your hands.
- Cook in fairly hot oven (190°C/ 375°F/ gas 5) for about half an hour. This cake is very good when cold.

Torta di mele
Apple cake

Ingredients for 6 people

- 5 large apples (Golden delicious)
- Plain white flour: 150 g/ 5 oz/ 1½ cups
- Sugar : 300 g/ 11 oz/ 1½ cups
- Pine nuts: 50 g/ 1¾ oz
- Butter: 100 g/ 3½ oz/ ½ cup
- Raisins or sultanas: 100 g/ 3½ oz
- 3 eggs
- ½ cup of milk
- 1 lemon
- Baking powder: 1 tblsp
- Salt

- Peel the apples, cut into four sections, remove the core and slice finely.
- Mix the softened butter with the sugar, then add the flour, the eggs, the milk, a pinch of salt and the grated lemon rind. Mix well, then add the pine nuts, the soaked raisins and the baking powder.
- Grease and flour an ovenproof tray 23 cm/ 9 inches wide and pour the mixture into this, sprinkle the surface with the apple slices and place in a hot oven (200°C/ 400°F/ gas 6) for about 45 minutes.

Torta di ricotta
Ricotta cake

Ingredients for 6 people

- Ricotta: 300 g/ 11 oz
- Plain white flour: 200 g/ 7 oz/ 2 cups
- Sugar: 200 g/ 7 oz/ 1 cup
- Butter: 100 g/ 3½ oz/ ½ cup
- Raisins: 50 g/ 1¾ oz
- 3 eggs
- 1 lemon
- Powered vanilla or vanillin
- Salt

- Prepare the shortcrust pastry by mixing together the flour, an egg, the softened butter, 100 g/ 3½ oz/ ½ cup of sugar and a pinch of salt; make a ball and leave to stand in the fridge for about half an hour.

- Mix the ricotta in a bowl with two eggs, the rest of the sugar, the soaked raisins, the vanilla and the grated lemon rind.
- Butter a baking tray, place the pastry in the middle and, using your fingers, spread this out to the edges, thus lining the bottom and sides. Pour in the ricotta mixture, level out and use the excess pastry around the edge to cover the ricotta.
- Cook in a moderate oven (175°C/ 350°F/ gas 4) for about half an hour.

Torta di riso
Rice cake

Ingredients for 6 people

- Rice (Italian Arborio): 300 g/ 11 oz
- Granulated (castor) sugar: 200 g/ 7 oz/ 1 cup
- Powered vanilla or vanillin
- Candied peel of orange and lime: 100 g/ 3½ oz
- Raisins or sultanas: 100 g/ 3½ oz
- Butter: 100 g/ 3½ oz/ ½ cup
- 3 eggs
- Milk: 1 litre/ 1¾ pints/ 4 cups
- 1 lemon
- Salt

- Put the milk, two cups of water, the sugar, the grated lemon rind and a pinch of salt in a pot. Bring to the boil and add the rice. Cook until all the liquid has been absorbed.
- Leave to cool, then, mixing all the time, add the eggs, the vanilla, the butter, the candied peel and the soaked raisins.
- Pour the mixture into a tray, greased well with a little butter; bake in a hot oven (200°C/ 400°F/ gas 6) for about half an hour.

Torta pinolata
Pine nut cake

Ingredients for 6 people

- Flour: 200 g/ 7 oz/ 2 cups
- Sugar: 200 g/ 7 oz/ 1 cup
- Butter: 150 g/ 5 oz/ ¾ cup
- Pine nuts: 100 g/ 3½ oz
- 1 egg
- 3 egg yolks
- Baking powder: ½ tblsp
- 1 lemon
- Salt

- Mix the sugar and butter (leaving a little to grease the baking tray) until creamy and smooth; add the flour, the eggs, the baking powder, a pinch of salt, the grated lemon rind and mix again.
- Pour this mixture into a buttered, floured baking tray and distribute the pine nuts evenly over the top.
- Cook in moderate oven (180°C/ 350°F/ gas 4) for about 40 minutes.

Zuccata
Pumpkin jam

Ingredients

- Pumpkin: about 3 Kg/ 6½ lb
- Sugar: about 1,5 Kg/ 3 lb

- Clean the pumpkin by removing skin and seeds, chop into large pieces and boil in water; drain well and leave to soak in cold water for a long time, changing the water occasionally.
- Dry the pumpkin in the open air (or in a warm oven) and strain through a sieve.
- Put this paste into a pot with its same weight in sugar and cook, stirring occasionally, until jam-like in consistency. This can be kept in glass jam jars.

This delicious jam was once very popular in Florence; today is has been totally forgotten.

Zuccotto
Ricotta bombe

Ingredients for 6 people

- Sponge cake: 250 g/ 9 oz
- Ricotta: 250 g/ 9 oz
- Whipping cream: 250 g/ 9 oz
- Bitter chocolate: 100 g/ 3½ oz
- Candied cherries and lime: 50 g/ 1¾ oz
- Granulated (castor) sugar: 100 g/ 3½ oz/ ½ cup
- Icing sugar: 150 g/ 5 oz/ ¾ cup
- Cognac or brandy: ¼ glass
- Sweet liqueur (Grand Marnier, kirsch or rum): ½ glass
- Bitter cocoa powder: 2 tblsp

- Whip the cream and sweeten with the icing sugar, then add the ricotta, having strained this through a sieve.
- Divide into two unequal parts; in the larger, add the chopped candied fruit and the chocolate in little pieces; in the smaller part mix the cocoa powder.
- Remove the crust and the edges of the sponge cake, then cut horizontally into two discs about 1 cm/ ½ inch thick, cut out a small disc to place in the bottom of a charlotte mould (like a large bowl, capacity 1,5 litres/ 2½ pints) and many rectangles to line the sides.
- Soak these with a mixture of the various liqueurs diluted with a little water.
- Cover the sponge cake with a layer of chocolate cream, then fill the mould with the rest of the white cream and cover the whole with sponge cake soaked in liqueur.
- Press down with a disc of greaseproof paper and place the zuccotto in the fridge for about 5 hours.
- Remember that real zuccotto should be a "semifreddo" (half-cold), not an ice-cream.

Basic information on key ingredients

Beans

The most commonly used beans (in soups and as a side dish) are fresh or dried white haricot beans. In Florence "cannellini" beans are particularly popular.

Red kidney beans (borlotti) are sometimes used in soups.

Bread

Tuscan bread (a large round loaf) is the base of Florentine recipes. It is called "pane casalingo" (home-made) or "pane di campagna" (peasant) or "pane integrale" (whole-wheat).

It is usually prepared with whole-wheat (1/3) and white unbleached flour (2/3). Whole-wheat should be stone-ground without bran or kernel.

Never use brown bread.

Try and find this bread which is essential for soups. For crostini and skewers you can also use a long white loaf similar to the French baguette.

Broth

Broth is usually used in braised dishes, stews, risotto, etc. In these, you do not need to prepare a real meat or vegetable broth, you can use a good quality bouillon (stock) cube dissolved in some hot water.

However for a good soup you should prepare the broth as suggested on page 61.

In broth never use pork, lamb, giblets, tripe, tongue or offal.

Flour

Italian flour is plain soft wheat white flour (without vitamins, baking powder, sugar, salt).

Mushrooms

Florentine recipes use only wild "porcini" or ceps (Boletus edulis). Do not use champignons. You can use dried porcini sold in little packets, which should be reconstituted by soaking in hot water for 15 minutes. Filter the water and use in cooking with the mushrooms.

Olive oil

Always choose Italian extra virgin olive oil. Do not use Spanish, Greek or French olive oil.

Pancetta

Pancetta is unsmoked slab bacon. You can substitute pancetta with bacon as long as it is not smoked.

Parmesan cheese

Always try to find whole pieces of real Italian "Parmigiano-Reggiano". Only use grated Parmesan in jars, plastic packets or loose if whole pieces are not available.

Pasta (Factory-made)

Always choose Italian "pura semolina" (durum wheat) pasta and cook in plenty of salted water. Drain when "al dente", in other words, slightly undercooked.

Rice

For "risotto" use the Italian Arborio or other top quality Italian rice. Do not use Chinese long grain varieties. For cakes and soups you can use Italian short grain varieties.

Ricotta

Ricotta is a soft fresh cheese made from whey, a watery ewes' milk residue.

Tomatoes

Always choose Italian canned plum tomatoes (with no added sugar).
Concentrated tomato purée (paste in a tube) can be used in some sauces and stews.

Vinegar

Always choose white or red wine vinegar (top quality). Do not use balsamic vinegar.

Index

Paolo Petroni was born and lives in Florence. Having taken a degree in Business Administration, he now runs his own company specializing in Marketing Consultancy and Research.

As a journalist, he writes articles on food and wine for national newspapers and magazines. He has written a number of successful books on cookery including "The Complete Guide to Fish Cookery" and "The Great Book of Tuscan Cooking" and is also co-author of several guides to Italian and Florentine restaurants.

Paolo Petroni is a councilor of the "Accademia Italiana della Cucina" and honorary Delegate of the Florentine Chapter.